Unto

Confidence

100% Proven Methods to Overcome Anxiety, Thrive in Your Relationships, Conquer Panic, Rapid Relief from Toxic Stress, Release Fear & Intrusive Thoughts

Written By

Carl Zimmerman

Carl Zimmerman

engaging in the rendering of legal, financial, medical or professional advice. The content within this book has been derived from various sources. Please consult a licensed professional before attempting any techniques outlined in this book.

By reading this document, the reader agrees that under no circumstances is the author responsible for any losses, direct or indirect, that are incurred as a result of the use of information contained within this document, including, but not limited to, errors, omissions, or inaccuracies.

Table of Contents

Introduction

Confidence. Everyone has it except for you. Your life would be so much better if only you had this magical, elusive thing called confidence. Do thoughts like these run through your mind on a daily basis? Are you searching for that elusive hack or trick that will boost your confidence to the stratosphere and create happiness and satisfaction in your life forever and ever?

Confidence, charisma, fearlessness, whatever you want to call it is one of the keys to success in life. There is no doubt about this. The world respects a person who is sure of themselves far more than someone who is possessed by doubt. What does true confidence look like, though?

Confidence permeates everything we do it affects our money, relationships, career, social interactions, and so on. This book aims to take a balanced look at what confidence really is and also give you a scientific context from which you can view things. All of us tend to get caught up with what's going on in our lives and sometimes, we forget that we are biological beings who have been engineered a certain way.

I don't mean to sound cold when I say this, but building confidence and charisma is a scientific process. Yes, there is emotion involved, but using your emotions in the right way is key to building confidence. Right now, you probably don't understand how to do this. Here's a quick test: Do you think fear is bad? You're probably thinking that in some cases it's justified. Well, how about anxiety? Now, we're in murkier waters. Let me muddy them further: Do you think depression is a valid sentiment?

These are the sorts of questions, among others, that this book will answer for you. In order to build confidence, you need to understand who you are and where you want to go. In order to go somewhere, you need to know what that looks like. Here's the catch though: Only you can define what that looks like. I can't tell you exactly what your ultimate destination needs to be.

The good news is that you already know all of these things. See, there isn't a cookie-cutter mold for confidence. Not every confident person is the same. You can be introverted and confident as much as a person can be extroverted and confident. You can be a loner and be secure with yourself or you can surround yourself with people and lack confidence.

A lot of confidence comes down to standards, and this is one of the areas I can guarantee you're struggling with. Your lack of confidence is not a disease, it is but a symptom of something missing in your life. Broadly speaking, this is usually a case of a lack of boundaries and standards.

How do you define good behavior? How do you tell someone they've crossed the line? How do you monitor yourself? Confidence is not about having the world perceive you in a different way as much as it is about changing your perception of yourself.

This is the biggest obstacle that people refuse to look at: You don't need to change the world. You need to change yourself. Self-examination will lead to all the answers you'll ever need.

How to Use This Book

This book is not one of those texts that is going to scream and shout at you. You know you have a problem, and you need to step up and deal with it. 'But it's so hard!' you might be thinking. Well, of course, it is. Why would you expect it to be easy? It's hard to build confidence. In other news, the weather gets cold in the winter and hot in the summer.

You'll start off by learning all about why a lack of confidence is a major problem for you. This isn't a motivational lesson but is a factual look at how our societies are changing and how the accelerated pace of change actually undermines confidence. We're dealing with a unique environment that no generation before us has had to deal with so in order to adjust, we need to first understand.

From there we'll move onto the biology of confidence. How does your brain work? How does it create your world and how can you make it work for you? After this, we're going to get into the meat of the book by looking at specific issues that cause a lack of confidence and how they debilitate you.

It isn't enough to just know what your problems are. You need to know what your destination looks like, and this is what the chapter on what confidence looks like will teach you. Following this, you'll learn about how you can get there via the last four chapters in this book, each of which addresses issues from a different point of view.

No matter where your issues lie, be it with your career or your romantic life or your social life, the underlying causes are the same. Instead of telling you exactly what's wrong, my aim is to teach you how to figure it out for yourself. After all, you're the only one you've got at the end of the day. This book will teach you to trust yourself more than anything else.

Which brings me to the most important point: This isn't a book you just read. You need to do the things that are mentioned here. Anyone can read a few lines, feel good about themselves, and then go on doing the exact same thing. If feeling good is all you're going to get out of this book, you're not going to make progress.

This book is about making you ask uncomfortable questions about yourself. You need to pause and think about what is being said and then go out and practice the exercises listed. You need to build habits. Otherwise, this book will be of no use. Ultimately, it is you who can make this book a success or a failure.

This is a very good thing. You don't need anyone except for yourself. You might not be able to see that right now, but trust me when I say this, you are more than capable of not only reaching where you want to go but exceeding that mental image of your ideal self you might have.

So buckle up because you're going to start a life-changing ride!

Chapter 1: Good Ain't Enough

Did you hear about Mike? Yeah, Mike was good at his job as a machine operator at the GM plant in Flint, MI. He was making good money, sent his kids to a good school, had a good home and a good life. Good, good, good and good.

Then the machines came and took his job. Poor Mike.

Good is an epidemic in this country at the moment. For the longest time, 'good' meant great thanks to the general prosperity that America witnessed after the world wars and the preeminent position of America's economy. This is no longer the case though, now it's adapt or die.

Change and Adaptation

Whether you realize it or not, we're living through the biggest upheaval humanity has ever witnessed. The digital and technological revolution that has taken place since the advent of the internet has meant that this generation of people has witnessed more change in half a lifetime than multiple generations that came before. (Ritholtz, 2017).

Think about how the humble telephone has changed. We went from rotary dials to buttons on landline instruments (remember those?). Then we went to the first cell phone which was a brick with an antenna sticking out of it. Then came the tiny cell phones with buttons on them. They flipped, beeped, and survived a three-story fall.

In less than a decade, they were replaced by the smartphone, and now, the thing you hold in your hand is more powerful than the computer that sent Neil Armstrong, Buzz Aldrin, and Michael Collins to the moon (Grossman, 2017). Society has changed rapidly and continues to do so as we speak.

It is now quite common for you to interact with a robot. What do you think an automated customer service phone line is? Don't even get me started on Siri and Alexa. We've had a millennium of sweat and money being the most important resources, now that gets replaced by data points, and we still aren't sure how this is going to work moving forward.

The ground shifting beneath your feet is a singularly disconcerting experience. It is perfectly natural that such conditions produce intense fear and uncertainty. In such an environment, is it any wonder that confidence levels plummet? After all, isn't confidence a product of certainty?

Given this fact, we have a major problem then. A lack of confidence not only hinders our quality of life, but it also hobbles one of the best survival mechanisms we have as a species.

Carl Zimmerman

Adaptation

Nature has given every species on this planet everything it needs to survive. One of these tools is the phenomenon of adaptation. This refers to a species' ability to survive in diverse environments and change its own characteristics to suit new conditions. Well, that's the biological process out of the way. What does this mean for you though?

Your ability to adapt is directly related to your ability to deal with and thrive in situations that are constantly changing. The world today is one of constant change as we've just seen. Things remain stable for lesser periods of time and thus constant adaptation is called for.

Change can occur in all forms: You may suffer from a crisis or you may have to deal with a range of choices that will force change onto you and so on. How well you adapt determines your level of success. what lies at the heart of adaptation, though? What is it that really underlines your ability to deal with change?

Well, let's think about this a little more. Change brings discomfort, and discomfort brings fear. So really, successful handling of change is all about facing your fears. What do you need to face those fears? Confidence, of course! Thus, successful adaptation is all about having the confidence that you're going to be okay no matter what happens.

This is an unnerving proposition for most people who lack confidence. If you're one of these people, you probably think of confidence as something that comes with competence. In other words, confidence needs to be validated by something outside of you. Well, this isn't the case. Think of it this way: When Tom Brady throws an interception, do you think his confidence in his abilities decreases? Does it increase? Does it stay the same?

The answer is obvious. The athlete that succeeds the most is the one that manages to keep his or her confidence levels high despite the results on the outside. This is the point about confidence that a lot of people who lack it, miss. They're going around searching for validation in the present moment.

You're never going to receive such validation from the outside. How can you? After all, the outside world and its set of conditions are constantly changing, so the premise upon which you build your confidence is not going to last long. Instead, you need to turn within. Confidence is something you need to have no matter the result.

This means even if you obviously screw up, you need to be confident in your abilities. I don't mean to say that you need to adopt an attitude of bravado or overconfidence. I'm talking more about a kind of quiet confidence that every successful person has. They don't need to shout about it, but you can bet that when the tough times come, they'll see it through.

Confidence is what builds resilience during tough times. Things may be tough right now and you might be exhausted and sad but deep down, you know you'll see it through and that you will be fine.

Self-Image

At the heart of this innate confidence is your self-image. Your self-image is a collection of beliefs and facts that you have wired into your brain. You'll learn more about how this wiring takes place in the next chapter. For now, though, let's look at the self-image a bit more in detail.

Your self-image begins with your beliefs, and your beliefs are things you've learned about the outside world as you've grown up. Children start forming beliefs from as young as the age of a few months old, and by the time they're five, most of their beliefs are already installed.

It stands to reason that if you learned a bunch of stuff in order to form beliefs then you can learn new stuff in order to form new ones. So why not learn new beliefs in order to create a new self-image? An image that says 'I am more than enough.' At the heart of your lack of confidence is your inability to build a supportive self-image of yourself.

You view yourself as being not very good at certain things, and this is why you struggle with confidence. For example, if you struggle in social situations, you have a self-image of someone who doesn't do well in such situations. Your brain automatically plays that recorded file in your mind's eye and you end up enacting what you believe.

Well, let's step outside your head for a moment and take a look at the world around us. Have you ever noticed the behavior patterns of newly born chicks of migratory bird species? They follow the usual baby-like behavior pattern of being dependent on a care giver, but when the time comes to migrate, they don't need any instructions on where to fly and when to pack up and leave ("How Do Birds Know How to Migrate?", 2015).

They just do it automatically. All animals in nature exhibit some form of survival mechanism when it comes to living (Bailey, 2018). No one knows how and where this comes from, but there's no denying that it exists. We see this in human beings too. Babies do not consciously know they're hungry but know that they need some form of nourishment when the time comes and they cry out for it.

A survival instinct is preprogrammed into all of us by nature. Animals instinctively know what they need to do to survive, and nature gives them the tools to do so. Whether the animal chooses to use it or not is a different question. Interestingly, every animal automatically uses it without thought. It is only in human beings where things become more complicated than the rest of the natural world.

Carl Zimmerman

As human beings, our definition of survival is different from that of a dog or a cat. Give a dog some food and company and it's happy. A human being needs things beyond this to survive. We need to live. If nature has given you a mechanism to survive, is it possible that it has given you a mechanism to thrive as well? The answer is a resounding yes (Maltz, 1974).

This is the creative instinct within all of us. If you're thinking 'but I'm not creative' well, you've been creating things your whole life without recognizing it. You're part of a species that creates automatically. Look around at the world we've made for ourselves. Sure, we've made mistakes in some areas, but overall we continue to improve the lives of ourselves and our fellow humans. Our lives are a lot better these days because someone once upon a time thought of something that would be a good idea to bring to life.

Human beings can invent, not just discover. You are a part of the species just as much as your dog is a part of its species. So it follows that you share the same qualities as the most successful people out there. It's just that you're not using those qualities as much as you should because you're not aware of them.

This lack of awareness is what has led you to build this incorrect self-image in your head of someone who lacks competence, and this manifests as a lack of confidence. Do you see how this is a completely wrong self-image to have?

16

* You've literally been given everything you need to succeed in life. If this doesn't make you confident that its possible for you to be successful, what else can?

Furthermore, if you already have the tools to succeed, then why do you need external metrics to validate you? Think of it this way: You already have the keys to success and your results. If you have the keys, isn't success guaranteed? So why do other people's opinions come into play? It is only if you believe that you don't have the keys, that you need someone else to validate you.

Hopefully, you can see what sort of a self-image you now need to adopt. You have been engineered for success, and if this is true, how does it reconcile with the unsuccessful or failure-prone stereotype you've built for yourself in your head? It doesn't. You have an amazing creative mechanism, and this guarantees your success by showing you the path you need to take.

Adopting the correct self-image will help you see the world in a new light. It will help you become more confident and, ironically, this is what will bring the outside results that will form a base for further increases of confidence. I'm not saying the outside results validate the inner confidence. It's just that the world will have more confidence in you, and this will reinforce your self-image of being someone successful.

Carl Zimmerman

Confidence is a vital part of success, but do you know how vital it is? Let's take a look.

Confidence is Critical

A common trope of the world that no longer exists is the worker who keeps her nose close to the grindstone and keeps putting out high-quality work with minimum fuss. This leads us to believe that if you keep focusing on the work, recognition will come and with it, the rewards of promotion and monetary gains.

Anyone who has spent even five minutes in the workplace will know what a bunch of lies this is. Yes, the quality of your work does matter over the long term, but without a little self-promotion, you're not going to get the rewards you deserve. In fact, the ones who do move forward in their careers tend to be the ones who promote themselves the most (Friedlander, 2017).

Such people tend to be overconfident when it comes to their own abilities. A study conducted in 2009 by a psychologist at the University of California at Berkeley, Cameron Anderson, provides fascinating reading (Friedlander, 2017). As a part of his class, during the beginning of the semester, Anderson gave his students a list of historical events and personalities and asked them to check off who or what they knew about.

The catch was that he mixed in some fake events and names in there as well. When tallying the number of items a student had checked off, Anderson found a direct correlation between the number of items and that student's overall confidence. The experiment doesn't end there.

Most distressingly for those who lack confidence, the students who had demonstrated the highest amount of overconfidence ended up achieving the highest social status in their peer group (Friedlander, 2017). Anderson measured social status as influence, respect, and prominence in their own social groups.

The results are pretty easy to translate to your average workplace. The ones whom your boss recognizes the most are the ones who display the most confidence. Their actual ability and results have very little to do with it. If anything, such people can get away with working less and producing less since any result simply validates the initial good impression that confidence causes.

This is a bit like the conundrum of it being more expensive to be poor while being cheaper to be rich. The poor, on average, pay higher fees for the services they use and spend their time dealing with things that decrease their ability to earn money while the rich often pay far less in fees and receive more freedom (Friedlander, 2017).

The people who are overconfident or just confident can get away with producing less than the ones who aren't confident of their abilities.

Confidence Sways

People who display confidence don't just use their words to make a point. They exhibit certain behaviors via their body language, their tonality, their ability to maintain the right amount of eye contact, and so on. These nonverbal cues are what we pick up on when interacting with someone we don't know very well.

Nonverbal cues are why 'fake it till you make it' doesn't work. Everyone has a really good lie detector within them, and this detector works off the signals provided by little nonverbal and behavioral ticks. These are unconscious mechanisms that emanate directly from your self-image. If you start conversations based on claims you can't back up, your self-image is going to become really uncomfortable and will seek to rein you back in.

This is what other people will pick up on eventually. Hence, the lesson is that your ability does matter, but in order to achieve the highest amount of gain, your confidence levels need to be slightly higher than warranted. There shouldn't be too much of a gap between the two. Too small and you're not going to be recognized. Too big and you'll be labeled a liar.

Studies show that almost every successful person overestimates what they can achieve instead of correctly estimating it (Tigar, 2018). There's a very good reason for this. Overconfidence, the right amount of it, causes your brain to activate its creative mechanism and find solutions that don't yet exist. Do this often enough and your brain learns to equate the right amount of overconfidence with success.

Women often struggle with confidence when compared to men. There are sociological and biological reasons for this (Tigar, 2018). Either way, there is no denying the fact that women tend to clam up when in an environment that is either indifferent or against them, and men tend to do the opposite and go on the offensive.

In addition to this, women also tend to question themselves a lot more and think a lot more about their decisions before putting them into play. I don't mean to portray men as a bunch of maniacs who love jumping off cliffs without looking and women as a bunch of nancies cowering in the corner.

The reality is that bridging the gap in the workplace between women and men is simply a matter of a slight difference in confidence. On average, an equally competent man will be that little more overconfident of his abilities than a woman, whose confidence will likely be at the exact level of her abilities or slightly less.

Smarter people tend to suffer from this affliction as well. Correctly evaluating your abilities is the most logical thing to do, and overconfidence strikes them as being irrational. All sorts of known unknowns and the prospect of unknown unknowns end up making themselves heard, and the result is a more realistic but less confident looking picture being painted.

So if you happen to be a highly intelligent woman, you've got two things working against you. Thankfully the gap isn't too large to bridge. When viewed rationally, all you need to do is take your original estimates and increase the positivity of your projections a few notches, and you'll be fine.

Rethinking Confidence

You probably have some perception of what confidence is. Often, those who read books like this fall into two broad camps. On one side, confidence is all about deriving it from the facts of the situation. For example, you're stuck in the wilderness, and there's a bear looking at you thinking you'd make a tasty sandwich. Well, logic states that you shouldn't try to fight the bear but run as fast as you can, or faster than the slowest person as the joke goes. Such people don't fare very well in less extreme situations.

When things are going wrong and some inspiration is needed, those people are the last person the group looks to for inspiration. Not coincidentally, such a person will never be promoted to a leadership position either thanks to their reliance on hard facts and data to support their confidence.

The remaining bunch of people think of confidence as a feeling. No matter what the facts may be, they think if they can't feel it within them, they can't be confident about anything. Think of the nervous student who has prepared extensively for an exam. He's completed practice tests and has reviewed the study material thoroughly over and over again. Yet, he just doesn't 'feel' the confidence flowing, so he's a nervous wreck.

The truth is that confidence is justified by the existence of either one of these things or even both. If you have a feeling that you can succeed at a task everyone is failing at, this is just as valid as if you've reviewed the facts and can clearly see that there's not much more you can do to prepare.

Of course, your feeling of ability needs to be backed up by evidence of some sort otherwise you're exhibiting the kind of overconfidence that leads to failure. Confidence has a few other elements to it besides being born out of facts or as a feeling, as we'll see now.

Self-Compassion

People who suffer from low confidence tend to judge themselves too harshly. Think back to how you reacted to a less-than-positive result from one of your tasks. Often this viewpoint comes from rigorous adherence to the facts of the situation. For such people, success or failure is binary, and this naturally results in them fluctuating between criticism and faint praise.

The key to developing confidence is to disassociate yourself from your results. Hence, instead of saying 'I failed' you need to think 'the experiment/task/etc. didn't succeed.' These are very different viewpoints to take. The former assumes complete responsibility, which is the right thing to do but also imprints a negative stereotype onto the self-conscious.

Often people do this because of the way they were brought up. We'll explore this more in the next chapter. Either way, removing yourself from the situation enables you to view it more objectively without your emotions clouding the process. By doing this, you can view the real reasons for failure and hence give yourself a chance to bounce back.

Don't be ashamed to make success all about yourself. A lot of 'rational' thinkers who classify themselves as high achievers judge themselves far too harshly over the success as well. You need to take the time to congratulate yourself. Not doing so is just stupid. Above all else, remember the Buddhist mantra to always be kind to yourself first.

This is a pretty unique take on selfishness since it states that only by taking care of yourself first can you take care of everything else. This is a pretty logical train of thought. Hence, go ahead and be selfish. Be kind to yourself and treat yourself well. The world is harsh enough so don't compound matters by adding to the difficulties you'll face by building obstacles for yourself.

Optimism and Pessimism

Optimism has reached dangerously high levels of exposure in self-help media. Everyone is now running around saying you need to be optimistic, and a lot of this stems from the law of attraction material that exploded in popularity a few years ago. I'm not interested in debating whether or not the law of attraction is valid.

Of far more interest to me is to use both optimism and pessimism as they're meant to be used. Pessimism is simply the prevalence of negative feelings, and this has been demonized completely by new age gurus (alleged gurus). Well, I think pessimism has its place.

You see, your self-image isn't a moron. I mean you're not a moron, so why would your self-image be one? Walking around with a smile plastered on your face trying to be 'optimistic' all the time is only going to result in your self-image telling you that 'all of this is B.S.' You can't trick your self-image into becoming someone you are not.

While the self-image can be crafted into something else, the ideal self-image is one that stays true to who you really are. Think of it as uncovering your true self-image instead of thinking of having to mold it into another form. Your true self-image is there underneath. You need to uncover it. The thing is that some people are just predisposed to view things in a way that makes them miserable.

Take Charles Bukowski, for example. He was a magnificent screw up by his own definition and couldn't seemingly muster an ounce of happiness to save his life. Was he miserable, though? 'Find what you love and let it kill you,' he famously said (Manson, 2013). If Bukowski was truly miserable, he wouldn't have been talking about finding passion and so on, I think.

There's a difference between accepting your inherent pessimism (if you happen to be predisposed toward it) and the pessimism that emanates from not staying true to who you are. The latter is a problem. The former will likely work in your favor as it did for Bukowski. He was radically honest about his pain and the damage it caused in his life, but to him, it was all worth it. He found what he loved, and it was killing him. Do you think it took confidence to open himself up to the world in such a painful way? I think so!

My point is that confidence isn't some dewy-eyed adoption of optimism. Instead of aiming for optimism, aim to figure out how you can stay true to yourself. If it means being miserable occasionally, so be it. Don't be one just for the sake of being one, though; that doesn't make any sense.

Confidence comes ultimately from the knowledge that you are yourself and that this is okay. Nothing more is needed and nothing more can add anything to your life. The exercises at the end of this book are all about this. Before attempting them, though, you need to understand the need to move beyond binary concepts like optimism or pessimism to develop confidence.

Chapter 2: Wired for Confidence

Are some people predisposed for confidence more than others? Is there such a thing as being born confident or is it a learned function? There are many myths in our society when it comes to talent and the effect it has on a person's overall results. Confidence is just one of those things that people seem to misunderstand, much like talent.

To fully understand the answers to these questions, we need to delve into our brains' physical structures and understand how they work. Hopefully, by the end of this chapter, you'll clearly see that a lot of what you've been told about talent and hard work is mostly incorrect.

Or perhaps you'll see that you've been believing the right things but haven't been putting them into practice the right way. So, having said that, let's jump in and dissect your brain.

The Brain

As far as internal organs go, the brain stands on an equal pedestal with the heart as being one of the two most important centers in our body. While the heart has a very definite physical function, which is to pump blood everywhere, the brain is a far more complex thing to understand. It has a mind of its own, quite literally.

I mean, when you think about it, the fact that we don't fully understand the way our brain works implies that our brains don't know how they work themselves. This sort of mind-bending phenomenon is quite common when it comes to studying the human brain, and it's easy to get lost in the various alleyways that exist.

My aim in examining the brain here is not to give you a biological lesson. Instead, I'm aiming to help you understand the basics of how it works and then move onto the important stuff of how you can get it to work for you. Believe it or not, the brain often works against us. This isn't because it's some spiteful creature. It's just that we feed it one thing, but it interprets it as something else.

First, we need to understand the brain from an evolutionary perspective.

Evolution

From an evolutionary standpoint, the brain can be divided into two portions: the less developed fast brain and the more evolved slow brain (Kahneman, 2011). The fast brain is sometimes referred to as the reptilian brain thanks to the resemblance of its organs in a reptile's brain. In fact, it goes beyond mere resemblance in some cases. We find that the human brain has the exact same organ functionality as a reptile's brain does (Kahneman, 2011).

This fast brain lies at the bottom of the cross-section of our brains. When thinking of the human brain we envision a bunch of soft tissue, but that's not what this portion of the brain is. This is the stuff that lies beneath all of that tissue. Given its name you might be wondering what is the point of having it in the first place?

Well, the reptilian brain performs a whole bunch of important functions. For one, it's what helps keep you alive, from a survival standpoint. If you're faced with any mortal threat, this is the portion of the brain that takes over and guides you to safety. For example, it is impossible for you to hold your breath and suffocate. This is because your reptilian brain simply overrides everything else and leaves you with no choice (while presumably thinking you're an idiot).

When this part of the brain assumes control of your body, it redirects a number of body functions toward its purpose. For example, if you're faced with a predator in your surroundings or something dangerous like a vehicle speeding toward you, it directs your heart to pump blood to your limbs to enable you to get out of the way.

It focuses your senses on the present moment and you literally lose the ability to think about anything else. All of your focus is on avoiding danger. Understand that this is not a reasoning process. You simply move to wherever danger isn't. You don't stand there thinking 'if I jump over the barrier, the vehicle is going to pass me by,' you just jump and then keep an eye out to see if you need to reassess the danger.

This is why it is referred to as the fast brain. It doesn't take time to think things over. Given its function, this makes perfect sense, and you want it to be this way. The trouble occurs when it starts butting into places it has no business being in. If you have stage fright, you've experienced the same feelings as the ones described above despite there being no physical threat to you whatsoever.

In such situations, we become paralyzed and unable to think clearly. This is because your brain has literally shut down and is focused only on avoiding the perceived threat. The only way to extricate yourself from this mess is to call upon the services of your slow brain.

The slow brain is the more evolved portion of our brain, and this is the mushy tissue that you think of in the image of a brain. It is made up of fatty tissue and water for the most part (Kahneman, 2011) and is capable of complex reasoning. Hence, it functions in a slow, more reasoned manner.

Despite all of the progress human beings have made over the years, we still can't figure out how to get along well with one another and how to use the two halves of our brain appropriately. Now, I'm taking a liberty here in describing these as halves, but this is to merely illustrate a point. Your slow brain has a set of conditions it excels in and your fast brain another set. Between the two of them, they're pretty powerful.

When the two sets of conditions get muddled up, you might as well be a squirrel for all the mental power you'll have at your disposal. So how do we decide which conditions warrant the slow brain or the fast brain? This is where your belief system comes into play.

Neural Networks

If the outer world and the experiences it throws at you is a stream of sunlight, your beliefs are the prism which split it into a spectrum. In this case, you can think of your beliefs as splitting your sensory inputs—that is whatever information you receive from your eyes, ears, nose, tongue, and skin—into two streams. One goes to your slow brain and one to your fast.

This is why it is very easy to misinterpret completely non-threatening experiences as life-threatening ones. Walking onto a stage or trying to approach a potential romantic partner come to be viewed as life-threatening events, and you end up sabotaging yourself because your beliefs lead you to interpret things all wrong.

As we saw in the previous chapter, your beliefs are simply the sum of your learned information gathered from your prior experiences. This information is stored deep inside your brain and hardened by years of usage. When I say hardened, I mean this literally.

You see, the way your brain stores information is truly unique. You might think that the brain is a filing cabinet, but this is untrue (Kahneman, 2011). In fact, your brain's storage system is more radial in nature and actually is a network. Each brain cell, called a neuron, contains a tiny bit of information and can form networks with multiple neurons at once. Hence, a single neuron can be part of multiple neural networks.

When these networks activate, what's happening is that one neuron is communicating with another via generating a tiny electrical current. Now, we are thrown a lot of information to handle in our lives, so how does our brain decide what is important and what isn't?

This is an extremely complex process that isn't fully understood biologically. As a matter of fact, we don't understand much about neural networks themselves or else we would have created one by now. What we do know is this: The brain seems to evaluate incoming information through the prism of existing beliefs and then evaluates it on the basis of how often this piece of information is used.

So if you learn to play the guitar, when starting off, your brain checks to see if it harms you in any way. If you were involved in a terrible accident with a guitar as a kid, it is unlikely to assist you in helping you learn how to play since your fast brain comes in and shuts everything down until you remove yourself from the guitar's presence.

If the guitar passes this test, a preliminary neural network is formed. It's still weak at this point, so you're likely to forget about it. However, with continued practice and action, the neural networks that correspond to guitar playing strengthen and thicken. As they become thicker, the more automatic they become. The more automatic they are, obviously, the less you have to think about what you're doing.

When you start out plucking strings and playing the G chord, you'll need to see how your fingers are placed, and you'll need to consciously think about their placement. Over years of practice though, it'll come automatically to you, and you won't give it a second thought. When a neural network strengthens, it gets removed from your conscious mind and is stored into your subconscious.

Your self-image also resides in your subconscious mind, and this is where all of your strongest beliefs and thoughts are held. The subconscious isn't a physical structure, mind you. It just refers to a collection of extremely strong, automatic neural networks. By its very definition, the actions that come from the subconscious are not thought about. In fact, for the most part, we aren't even aware of what we're doing.

I mean, when was the last time you thought about brushing your teeth in a conscious manner? You brushed, spat, rinsed, and moved on, all the time thinking of how you're going to make it to work on time. In other words, you're completely confident about brushing your teeth well. You've done it so many times, you're competent enough to do it automatically.

Competence really equals a strong neural network. The stronger it is, the more competent you are. Of course, for a neural network to form in the first place, sensory input needs to pass through your belief system first. Once it passes this, it proceeds to get installed. So this begs the question: How do behaviors get installed? In other words, how do you learn something?

Learning

When you were a small child, you were forced to memorize a lot of things in kindergarten. One of the things you meticulously memorized was the alphabet. You even learned it in a sing-song way to trick you into thinking you were learning something, awesome but really it was just a string of letters.

Such sorcery was not possible when it came to numbers though. Here you had to memorize what the numbers looked like and how they combined to form other numbers. Then there were multiplication tables which were probably a special kind of torture if you didn't memorize them correctly.

In light of all this learning trauma, what if you could go back in time and teach your little self some shortcut to learning all this stuff? Does a Matrix-style plug and learn system exist? Well, unfortunately not. However, there are ways to speed up the learning process, and this involves maximizing the factors the brain takes into account when learning.

The first and most obvious factor is focus. The more attention you pay to the thing you want to learn, the faster you learn it. This is why your teacher played all sorts of tricks on you when getting you to learn things. They taught you a pleasant-sounding song to get you to focus on learning the lyrics. As a result, you learned your ABC's. They gave you rewards so that you used that incentive to focus on getting things right. In some cases, they even used the threat of negative incentives (punishment) to get you to focus on a task.

This leads us to the second important thing when it comes to learning and that is emotion. The carrot and stick approach works because either option generates emotions within us, and these provide incentives for us to learn something. If you loved smacking a ball with a bat or chucking a ball at things, this gave you additional incentive to learn more about baseball or other similar sports, if running provided a positive almost meditative state you would be incentivized to look into track and field type activities.

Note that emotion doesn't need to be positive or negative; you'll learn something either way. It's just that if you want to do something, you should try to associate positive emotions with it. If you want to avoid something, you need to associate negative emotions with it. The methods of Alcoholics Anonymous and those who quit smoking use the power of emotions to override old habits and create new ones. They keep reminding themselves of the negative effects these habits have on their lives, they try to quit these habits and build new habits that generate positive emotions.

Despite all the focus and emotion in the world, you couldn't quite learn your ABC's the first time. You had to repeat them over and over again until it was ingrained in your mind. This is nothing but brute force repetition. Truth be told, repetition by itself is more than enough to learn. Even if you hate numbers, you probably know what 1, 2, and 3 look like unprompted. You know basic multiplication tables even if they were of no interest to you. Repetition is a necessary evil and is the most effective way of learning something.

The last component is a more imprecise one and deals with intentionality. Your intention behind learning something has two components. First, you need to clarify that it is your intention to learn the information, and second, you need to give yourself a good reason as to why this is your intention. This ties back to the emotion factor in learning.

For example, you want to learn French. Prior to a lesson, you remind yourself that the reason you're putting yourself through all the grammatical torture is that you want to learn French. Why? Well, the positive emotion you'll feel when those pretty French girls bat their eyelids at you makes it worthwhile. Intentionality infuses everything you do when it comes to learning. Without this, you'll constantly wonder why on earth you're doing something and it makes things much harder.

So now that you have a picture of how learning occurs, how does it all tie back to your confidence levels?

Success and Failure

The confidence you have when it comes to carrying out certain actions is simply a reflection of what you have learned with regards to that scenario. What you have learned is nothing but your belief system. If you feel a lack of confidence, this simply means you have learned an unsupportive set of beliefs about that particular situation. If you're frightened out of your mind when you need to speak to a group of people, you've learned something about group scenarios that is not supporting you.

If you learned something once, can you learn something else to replace it? Of course, you can! Using the power of intentionality, emotion, focus, and repetition, you can replace and re-educate yourself. This is how new habits are formed (Kahneman, 2011).

When you set the intention to learn something new, you're allowing some sensory input to pass through your belief system. Without the intention, your belief system would have filtered it out completely. Now, there's a fledgling neural network inside your head. It needs nurturing via focus, emotion, and repetition.

However, in addition to this network, you also have a much stronger, opposite neural network, and this is going to fight back and assert dominance. This is where focus and emotion are so important. You need to remind yourself of why the old belief system is wrong and how it has negatively impacted you. Then, you focus on the new habit and carry it out. Repeat it over and over, and you'll deactivate the older belief system and strengthen the new one.

When it comes to particular habits, this is a very powerful technique. However, for those who suffer from a general lack of confidence when it comes to a lot of things, there are deeper beliefs that need to be uninstalled. I'll address these in the next chapter under the section Limiting Beliefs, but before that, there is a preliminary belief that you're likely carrying around which is harming you.

This has to do with the importance of talent and how it relates to hard work.

Does Talent Matter?

We're faced with many situations in life where we have to go up against a person to whom everything seems to come naturally. If you work at a highly skilled job, there's likely that one person who is a bonafide genius and who seems to grasp everything the minute it's put down. You, on the other hand, fumble around struggling to make heads or tails of it.

Another common scenario is within our romantic lives where you often see that one person who attracts everyone like flies to honey without seeming to exert any effort. All the while you feel like Quasimodo and just can't muster the courage to go talk to people. They must be born with it, you mutter, and justify the state of things.

Telling ourselves that someone is born with something is a huge lie we tell ourselves. Perversely, uttering this lie makes us feel good because it justifies why we're helpless in the situation. You hear the word talent all the time in sports. Peyton Manning was the most talented QB coming out of high school, was the most talented NCAA QB to enter the NFL, and ended up winning two Super Bowls thanks to his immense talent.

If he was really that talented, what was the need for Manning to practice for multiple hours every day for close to three decades to the point where he lost feeling in his fingers, one wonders (Schilken, 2015)? The truth is that talent doesn't count for much in the overall scheme of things.

Sure, at an elite level, it creates a marginal difference. However, the lesser-talented person who loses out is also at an equally elite level and can hardly be labeled a failure. Justifying an inferior position for yourself because of a lack of talent or because you tell yourself you weren't born with it is an invalid excuse.

Research conducted by Dr. Carol Dweck of Stanford University shows that more than talent, it is hard work that wins the day (Dweck, 2016). In her best-selling book, *Mindset*, Dr. Dweck deeply discusses the importance of adopting an attitude of constant learning and a belief system that supports the importance of hard work over talent when it comes to success.

The message is pretty clear. If you're lacking confidence in something, you're telling yourself the wrong story in order to make yourself feel more comfortable in the short term. Never mind that this makes you miserable over the long term. You see, some people really are wired for success and the confidence that comes along with it.

They're the ones who believe they can create their own success and that this can be done through hard work. They know how to use the four boosters of learning and utilize it repeatedly until they get good at what they want to achieve.

Goals

So what do you want to achieve? Well, in the context of this book, confidence is as good a goal as any. The thing to realize is that your goal is an outcome. It defines a state of existence where something is occurring in your life. However, you should not focus on the goal exclusively.

What you ought to focus on instead is the process that materializes that outcome. You want to gain confidence, but it isn't enough to walk around all day muttering 'confident, confident' to yourself. This is only going to make you look like a psycho. Instead, you need to take action and develop a plan. Then you need to work hard at it.

This is why the law of attraction and other new age spirituality doesn't work for a lot of people. Individuals who simply believe in the principle and walk around feeling good all the time without taking action are no different from you muttering to yourself. So, in addition to having a goal (outcome), you need to have a plan of action with process-related milestones (goals).

Your process-related goals could be anything from executing a portion of your plan to developing a new plan of action. The point is that everything to do with this milestone is in your hands. If you want a raise at work, you need to start presenting yourself better so that your boss trusts you. You can control this.

You can control the quality of your work. You can control your interactions with your co-workers. You can control the level of kissing up you'll need to do to get ahead (sad but true). Can you control whether your boss will say yes or no? No, you can't. But that's an outcome and that's out of your hands anyway. Control the things you can by implementing an action plan and the outcomes will have a higher probability of becoming a reality.

Before we get into the ins and outs of developing a plan of action, let's first take a look at some of the causes of a lack of confidence. Keep the information you've learned in this chapter in your mind since this will be crucial for you to understand these behaviors as well as change them.

Chapter 3: What Causes a Lack of Confidence?

There are a number of things that cause a person to lose confidence in themselves. Most of them can be grouped under the large umbrella of limiting beliefs. Dealing with these beliefs is no easy task, but you have a framework you can use to defuse them. In fact, I'll expand on methods to defuse limiting beliefs in the final chapter.

This chapter is more about getting you to look at yourself and examine your high-level beliefs about success and failure. In addition, you'll also learn about one particular thing that you must change if you want to generate positive beliefs and confidence in your life.

Limiting Beliefs

There is no end of limiting beliefs in this world. It is impossible to list out every single one of them, but the ones listed here are high-level ones, and you will find that some of your specific beliefs will be a subset or a relation to of one of these.

If you spot a belief you're currently carrying, don't despair. Instead, congratulate yourself for having uncovered it and having become aware of it. Awareness is an extremely powerful tool and by shining a light on that belief, you'll now be on the lookout for when it asserts itself.

In other words, awareness is what enables you to move the belief from the subconscious to the conscious mind. You are more than capable of controlling your conscious mind and thus, control over your beliefs will soon follow.

#1- My Abilities Are Set in Stone, as Is My Potential

This is the talent versus hard work belief we looked at previously. If there is one belief that has caused more anguish than this one, I'm not aware of it. This is such a hopelessly disempowering belief that it is a tragedy so many people would be willing to adopt such thoughts. Yet, they most certainly do.

How do you know if you have this belief? Well, look back over your life and examine your behavior over the years. What sort of people are you attracted to and what do you think is the cause of success or failure? When you read a story of someone who recovered after a major setback, what are your thoughts? Do you think their success was set in stone or preordained? Or do you think they had to work for it?

You might argue that they always had the ability to perform at a high level and that it was just a few bad choices that removed them from their deserved position. In other words, their natural-born talent was waiting to be fulfilled, and their setback was a temporary anomaly. It's informative to turn to the NFL again in order to see how nonsensical this argument is.

Two of the best quarterbacks in the NFL, and indeed all time, play for the Patriots and the Packers. You might have heard of them: Tom Brady and Aaron Rodgers. Brady's story is now legendary, and even if you aren't a football fan, you've likely heard of it. Here's a guy who went from being the backup quarter back of a high school team that went 0-8 to a true sports legend, with six Super Bowl rings and a supermodel wife (O'Malley, 2017). His story needs no retelling.

Rodgers, though, is a great case study as well. He's universally viewed as the most naturally talented passer in the league, but this narrative conveniently ignores all the criticisms that have been thrown at him over the years. Indeed, all this 'talent' talk started right after he managed to win his first Super Bowl and everything that happened before was conveniently swept under the rug.

Let's start with his high school record. Despite having great stats, he was not recruited by a single Division 1 college. He was rejected by Florida State and received a walk-on place on the team from Illinois. He considered quitting football but was recruited by the local junior college and played for them for a year, aptly setting another bunch of records.

Around this time, the coach of the University of California, Jeff Tedford, swung by to take a look at the tight end on the team but ended up recruiting Rodgers instead. Rodgers and Cal set the Pac-10 on fire two years later, losing their only game to the powerhouse USC team. Rodgers was a consensus first-round pick (Demovsky, 2017).

However, on the day of the draft, no one picked him. What was most embarrassing was that Rodgers was forced to sit in the green room with the cameras rolling, with team after team passing him by. He fell all the way to 24th to Green Bay, a long drop for a guy who was expected to go first overall. This was just the beginning of his nightmare.

He was the backup to a legend in Green Bay, and after two years of being ignored, he finally received his chance to start, only for the legend to come back and try to reclaim his spot after going into retirement. The fans booed Rodgers that season relentlessly, and he was viewed as the inferior choice right up until he won his first Super Bowl.

Rodgers has since been named the league MVP twice and is the last person any defense in the league wants to face, when Green Bay is within a score and there's a play left. He is the NFL's 'Hail Mary' king, and this expertise comes thanks to the fact that he practices it regularly (Demovsky, 2017).

So, the most 'talented' QB in the league who chucks 80-yard bombs for fun has had to work physically and mentally for his success every step of the way. If Rodgers had placed his confidence on outside factors, he wouldn't have even played college football, let alone the NFL. While he has never explicitly mentioned it, it is laughable to think that Rodgers believes his abilities are set in stone or fixed in any way.

Indeed, a simple comparison of the way he used to play in college versus how he plays now is more than enough to see the difference hard work has had on his game and how much he has improved.

#2- Money Is Bad

This is a big one since it affects every single thing in your life. Your lack of confidence might not stem directly from money but could be caused by one of the side effects of you handling money improperly. Money remains a nuisance for most people thanks to the way we're brought up.

Growing up, we hear all sorts of statements about money and about rich people. The predominant views of money these days, in fact, show the degree of negative beliefs people have about money. Money by itself isn't good or bad. It's just a commodity that you transact in. It's no different from the coffee you drink to wake yourself up in the morning.

Solving issues with money requires you to go deep and examine everything in your life. How do you know if you have problems with money? Well, look at your results in this area. If you have none or if your financial life is extremely up and down, you likely have problems evaluating money in the correct manner.

The thing is, no matter how much I go on about how money isn't an emotional thing and is instead just a resource, you're liable to go out and keep making the same mistakes. This is because money is a deeply emotional issue for most people, unlike the previous limiting belief which is more of an intellectual one.

Money is directly connected to pain or pleasure for people thanks to the things it can buy. Separating the things you buy from money is an essential step to take. Here's a good way to test yourself: Lay down a $1 bill on the table. What do you think of it? Probably not much. You think that it can't buy you a lot of stuff. If someone were to walk in and steal it from under your nose, you're not going to like it, but you can live with it.

Well, what if someone laid down a million $1 bills on the table. What do you think of it then? It's the same $1 bill but just in greater quantity. Why does the greater quantity have a much bigger effect on you than a solitary bill? Probably because you're thinking of everything it could buy you.

Here's the thing: Studies show that beyond a certain threshold that everyone needs in order to live comfortably, earning more money is not going to make you happy. Money can make you happy but only up to a certain point. Beyond that, other things take over. This threshold is surprisingly low for someone living in the Western world. It works out to around $80,000 per year per person (Mack, 2019).

At this level, your basic needs are all taken care of and you have enough left over to spend on some of your wants. So, going back to our example previously: If someone were to walk in and steal the one million $1 bills from you, how would you react?

The key to resolving your issues with money lies in educating yourself and working out your emotional problems. With regard to emotional problems, the exercises in the final chapter will help you transform your beliefs about not just money but anything else that holds back your confidence.

The knowledge and educating part of the issue is resolved easily. Simply listen to wealthy people talk about money. You won't find a single one of them talking about how much they made. Instead, every single one of them focuses on either the process they use to make money or are focused on some other goal. Beyond their threshold, money doesn't matter anymore.

Warren Buffett, the billionaire owner of Berkshire Hathaway, is a prime example of this. The man is one of the richest people in the world and yet he's pledged his fortune away to Bill Gates' charity. He draws an annual salary of $100,000 and pays taxes on that amount. He still lives in the same house he purchased back in the 1960s in Omaha, Nebraska, which is the town he grew up in. The greatest investor who has ever lived pays his bills with a $100,000 pre-tax salary. So how much money do you really think you need?

Don't get me wrong, my point is not to say that chasing money above $100,000 is wrong. Far from it. My point is that you should figure out what your threshold is and then work to achieve it. Recognize that beyond that threshold, money doesn't mean so much to you and is more like your personal score card than a necessity.

You need money to live a comfortable life. No one likes living in a sweaty shared house with twenty other people in it, no matter how amazing they are. Everyone has needs and you need money to meet them. Examine your life and check your attitude toward money.

Often a lack of money manifests as a secondary lack of confidence.

#3- Religious and Cultural Beliefs

The culture and religions we grow up with have perhaps the deepest hold over us since they're forced upon us without our consent or choice. Often, we don't even realize that we can reject them until we reach adulthood. A lot of this is done with the best of intentions by our care givers, but the fact remains that what fits one person is not guaranteed to fit another.

Religion and the beliefs it proliferates can cause a lot of problems around confidence for a person even if they have left that framework behind. I'm not saying that religion causes a lack of confidence. Just that it creates it in certain areas. Many people who believe in the fact that a certain God gives and takes are going to have a hard time taking responsibility for their actions.

This could lead to a feeling of uncertainty when it comes to making decisions, especially if a lot of them have gone unfavorably. They'll ask themselves twice if they're doing things acceptably as God intends or whether the belief system is appropriate to begin with and so on.

These things happen in all sorts of settings not just the religious, but one of the starkest examples of this is kids who grow up in poor households then grow into adults who carry inferiority complexes when it comes to social interactions.

Most poor households are light on cash, and leisure is a luxury.

Even if the child grows into a prosperous adult, there are feelings of guilt or insecurity around people who are seen as being from a social class that is above them (Boghani, 2017). This is not a universal phenomenon; I'm just highlighting a common and fairly obvious example.

The key with these is to again recognize that such beliefs were not your choice and that they were thrust upon you. You learned this from your elders who learned it from their elders and this goes all the way back hundreds or even thousands of years. So really, you're copying the behavior of your ancient ancestors.

Examine how these beliefs impact your life and understand that you don't need to give them up, that's your choice. You just need to frame them better; they must be rooted in reality. The exercises in the final chapter will help you do this.

Environment

It is a proven fact that you are the sum of your environment. The people around you and their beliefs end up becoming yours. It follows that if you're hanging around people who are not confident, you'll end up reflecting their behavior.

Carl Zimmerman

Environment doesn't include just the people you hang out with but the media you consume as well. The way social media is structured these days, you'll be fed a diet of things that take you farther down the rabbit hole steeped in confirmation bias. This lack of alternate feedback is a real problem and leads to the sort of echo chamber type of thinking you see in mass media these days.

So what are some of the things to watch out for? The following sections will give you a map of the hotspots that go a long way in determining the quality of your environment.

Family and Friends

This is the big one. We spend most of our time interacting with these sets of people. If your family happens to be a large group of confident people, you're likely not the person reading this book. Family can have unintended consequences as well. People with more successful siblings often get marginalized unintentionally and often, there's no place to hide from continuous judgement.

Despite your family and siblings not intending to hurt you, they can cause pain nonetheless when they unconsciously behave in a certain manner. The same applies to your friends. So how do you generate confidence in such situations? Well, it's pretty easy with friends. If you have a group of people who belittle you or make you feel worse about yourself, cut them out of your life immediately. These people aren't your friends anyway.

You can't cut family away like this without causing mountains of drama for yourself. So the best thing to do is to marginalize them. If the pain they're causing you is unintentional, then examine your own behavior. Perhaps you're playing a certain role when around them?

We grow up adopting a certain position in the household, and this extends into adulthood without us realizing it. If you experience the same sort of negative emotions you experienced as a child, odds are that you're framing yourself in the same position. Recognize that this isn't true anymore and work your way out of it by using the learning framework.

Modeling

No, I'm not talking about appearing in ads. I'm referring to our tendency to model our behavior along the lines of those we admire. Everyone has a certain pattern, and when you dig deeper, you'll find that a lot of your behavior is based on the behavior of someone or something you admire.

Ask yourself what sort of shows do you watch? What media do you consume? What kind of stories appeal to you?

The answers to these questions will lead to a bunch of limiting beliefs about yourself. I don't mean to say that all media you consume will be negative. For example, you might have found Ragnar Lothbrok the Norse Viking hero to be a badass for some reason. Why was this? If you suffer from a lack of confidence do you think you're looking at something that he does? Are you living vicariously through him?

Gender-Specific Issues

It is a fact that men and women face certain issues the other sex does not face. Of course, this isn't taking into account the issues trans people face. How about those who identify as gender neutral? Everyone lives in a different world, so it is impossible to know and fully appreciate what the other person is going through.

As much as we would like our world to become equal, as long as at least two sexes exist, there's going to be disagreement and limiting beliefs placed on either sex. What makes it tough is that there is often no way to have the other side experience the reality that the affected party is going through.

While women face a lot of expectations and standards in society that are unfair, men face similar challenges. Not fulfilling those standards often leads to a severe lack of confidence which can dent even the strongest person. So let's take a look at some of the issues the sexes face.

Note: I'm discussing men and women here but do not take this to mean I'm ignoring the issues of people outside these two sexes. It's just that the themes of either sex carry over and hence most issues tend to be covered.

Issues Women Face

Frankly, the list of things women do not have to contend with will be a lot shorter than the things they have to deal with. The point about using internal metrics to measure self-worth is quite apt for women since they tend to be compared at face value right from a young age.

It is a fact that women struggle more with self-confidence than men in the workforce (Friedlander, 2017). A famous study published in the *Mckinsey Quarterly* in 2008 shows alarming gaps in confidence between female and male executives. The results showed that male applicants applied for a post when they met only 60% of the qualifications necessary, whereas women applied only if they felt they had 100% of the qualifications that the post required.

In short, women tend to be bigger perfectionists than men. This isn't so hard to understand since from a young age, girls are pressured to appear a certain way or face rejection. Girls are bombarded with images of perfection that they need to live up to, and this leads to serious issues in confidence.

Judgment is also dealt out pretty easily and in an unsolicited manner when it comes to women's behavior. A woman behaving a certain way invites more judgment than a man acting contrary to stereotypes (Friedlander, 2017). Comparisons are a daily part of life for young girls, and this extends naturally into adulthood.

Further compounding the issue is that traditionally feminine values are not seen as being leadership worthy. When we think of leaders, we envision qualities such as bravery, assertiveness, taking control, and so on. These are traditionally masculine values, and women are led to believe that leadership roles are better suited for men. The lack of role models doesn't help either.

Thankfully, this state of affairs is changing and women are holding their own in traditionally masculine areas like the military and construction. However, this is just the Western world, and when looked at worldwide, the issues women face are far worse. There are many countries where religious and cultural edicts force women into subservient roles.

All of this creates an atmosphere of persecution when viewed in an imbalanced manner, and this also undermines a woman's confidence. A feeling of how fragile everything is pervades, and there is also the feeling of first-world privilege that arises in women in the West when comparing their situations with those of women in more repressive regions of the world (Friedlander, 2017).

There are no easy fixes for this, and it will take time, but a good place to start is by fixing internal metrics to measure one's self-worth. Things such as looks, agreeability, and the ability to conform need to be discarded for higher goals as the chapters later in this book will explain.

Issues Men Face

It is easy to overlook the fact that men face a lot of issues along with women. While women's issues tend to receive a lot more coverage, understandably, thanks to the historic nature of things that are male-dominated. Male issues tend to be under-reported or even swept away and treated as being irrelevant.

This happens again thanks to gender stereotyping, which requires men to be strong and invulnerable. Any show of feelings or emotions is regarded as weak. We're long past the days when invading armies used to commit genocide as a matter of routine, but this sort of thinking still prevails.

Most alarmingly, men are more likely to dismiss male-related issues than women are. The biggest sources of male-related issues deal with resources, such as money and success. Society short changes both boys and girls in this regard because girls are not expected to fend for themselves since they can 'always find a man' while boys have to learn how to deal with things and become prosperous.

Hence, the world is always a bit harsher toward boys and young men since this is viewed as being a rite of passage, the tough path to success. Ironically, this is why most men tend to have higher confidence level, because at every stage of their lives, they've been called idiots, morons, and douchebags (Dweck, 2016). Witness a normal interaction between boys in the 11- to 14-year-old age bracket, and you'll see the painful truth in this.

Whether all of this is fair or unfair is beside the point.

We need to deal with our problems, face them and step into a stronger self-image.

Chapter 4: What Confidence Looks Like

So you want to be confident and think that if you were more confident your life is going to get better by a country mile. Great! So what does confidence look like? It is at this point that people usually go down the wrong path because they have some ideas about what it is but don't actually know how to spot it.

This mistake is understandable. After all, how can you know what something is when have never experienced it. It's a bit like asking someone who has never been to Europe to describe Paris. Sure, they'll get a few facts right, but can they really tell you all about what it's like to live in Paris or what springtime in Paris feels like?

It is very important that you understand the right signs of being confident, because nothing will derail your progress faster than adopting an incorrect role model. There's no shortage of people who project confidence in popular culture but are actually the most deeply insecure people you can find.

At the outset, let me make one thing very clear. Power, or the assumption of it, is not the same as confidence. Some of the world's leaders, both current and historic, have been deeply insecure people. I'm not talking just about The Donald, by the way.

Developing the right kind of confidence will help you figure out what works for you. Ultimately, confidence really is all about being comfortable with yourself. Let's begin by looking at some specific situations and then try to decode what that ultimate expression of confidence, really means.

Money

As we've seen, money is an important part of our lives, and any scarcity in this regard wreaks havoc on our confidence. This is more-true of men than of women thanks to societal expectations of men to be providers and bread winners. This view is changing, but when looking at things on a macro level, this stereotype holds.

There are people who are extremely good with money. I'm not talking just about the rich people of this world who are great at making it. I'm also including those who may have limited incomes but still manage to have money to pay for their wants and live content lives. While the ability to make oodles of money requires confidence, what being good with money ultimately comes down to is your ability to manage it. I mean, lottery winners receive a lot of money but hardly any of them manage to hang onto it (Dweck, 2016).

So what does money confidence look like? There's a simple framework to understand this. Simply look at a person's A, E, I, O, and U.

A- Ask for Help

People who are confident with their money don't hesitate to ask for assistance with managing it. These are the people who seek out financial advisors and then do what they're advised. They understand their circle of competence, as Charlie Munger puts it.

Asking for help should not be confused with going out and asking people to borrow money. People who are confident at managing their money reduce liabilities and bad debt relentlessly and do not look to take on debt unless it is a special circumstance. I've already highlighted the case of Warren Buffett in the previous chapter.

Well, if you study Buffett's life, you'll realize that the man has studiously avoided debt in all forms in his personal life. He avoided it to the extent that he only bought his own house when his wife finally had enough and the Buffetts ran out of space in their rented home. Even then, Buffett did not draw a mortgage on his home. He paid for it in cash.

This sort of behavior is the antithesis of the American Dream. Earning a salary and buying a home is a rite of passage. Yet notice how Buffett had the confidence to go against that popular advice. He did this in the 60s too, when financial advice was far more conservative.

The lesson from this is that financially confident people understand what they know inside and out. If they don't know something, they ask for help.

E- Educate

You will find that people who manage their money well are constantly educating themselves on how to do it better. See, their aim isn't just to manage money but to change their mindset with regards to it. As mentioned earlier, money is just a commodity. You might intellectually see the point of this statement, but do you understand it as well as you think you do?

A financially confident person would pause at that question and test themselves. They would then go out and educate themselves on whatever the results of that test are. Every good money manager started out as someone who knew nothing about money. The difference between them and you (if this is your affliction) is education.

They aren't afraid of saying 'I don't know' and then going ahead and figuring out how they can know the answer to such a question. Knowledge is power.

I- Invest

No one can get rich or live comfortably without investing in some form or another. I don't care what it is, the stock market, real estate, a business, your aunt's cat grooming salon, whatever it is. Money sitting as cash in the bank is useless, and financially savvy people understand this.

They understand that inflation ensures that whatever cash sits there is literally losing its value. This doesn't mean they have zero cash. It's just that they take a more balanced view of it. They have enough to cover their essentials and emergencies and some luxuries but no more than that.

The rest of it is out there circulating and increasing in value. This involves taking calculated risks which I'll talk about later. However, managing your money is more than just letting it sit there in a savings account. A financially confident person knows how to compare interest rates and has learned how to compare real rates of return.

Depending on how wealthy they are, they've even mastered the art of evaluating opportunity costs, which is the real secret of getting rich. Don't know what this is? Well, go out there and learn!

O- Own Assets

Do you know what an asset really is? You probably know what a liability is. It's something that costs you money or loses value. A car is a liability. However, it is a necessary one for most people. Can a liability like a car be turned into an asset? Why, of course! If your car manages to earn you more money than it loses, it is an asset.

This could involve selling ad space or using it for business or whatever. People who are confident with money take this a step further and extend this thinking to assets. If a liability can be turned into an asset, can an asset turn into a liability through carelessness?

Buying a home is a prime example. Unless you have a special need to live in a particular area (I mean a need, not a want) or some other special circumstance, there is no earthly reason for you to own a home and then live in it. There, I said it. This is because you're incurring a massive opportunity cost even if your home increases in value.

This isn't a financial book, so I'm not going into the details. My point is: educate yourself. Understand what an asset really is. Here's a good rule of thumb: An asset is something that increases your wealth and freedom. By freedom, I mean a reduction of worry for your mind. Financially confident people understand this concept backward.

U- Understand Risk

Risk scares the life out of most people who are not confident with money. Those who understand money adopt a more balanced view. Your money needs to grow in order to have any value. This means you need to adopt risk. So what is your risk profile? How much can you stomach? Before you rush to answer them, I must confess: These are trick questions.

The concept of a risk profile will only leave you tangled trying to figure out which way is up. Instead, do what financially confident people do and adopt a reward to risk model. How much will you get back for the amount you put in? Can you afford to put that much in? If yes, do it. If no, can you do it with a smaller amount? Simple and easy.

Looking at things from a reward to risk standpoint is a natural by-product of understanding opportunity cost. You might put a down payment on a home of $50,000 for a twenty-year mortgage that is going to result in your paying 1.5X your home's current value over that period of time. Let's say the lords of Wall Street don't create another crisis over this time period and your home increases in line with historic values. You'll probably realize an effective gain of 4-5% compounded over that time. So 4-5% over 20 years.

Well, what if you took that $50,000 and started a business that could generate $10,000 per month within six months? Would you make that deal? What's the risk? Can you mitigate it? How can you do that? How does it compare to your other option?

Welcome to the reward to risk model of thinking. Here's an interesting question for you to ponder since we're here: What's the biggest risk inherent in the home-buying option? We're assuming your home is going to increase in value, so it's not a decrease of capital value.

Answer: The opportunity cost of foregoing another income stre

Career

The workplace is an area where every one of us could use some more confidence. All the way from interviewing to asking for a raise, your level of confidence in the workplace determines a lot of things for the rest of your life. So let's take a look at what confidence in the workplace looks like.

Track

People who are confident with their careers have this quality because they know exactly where they are and where they're headed. By tracking their career progress and creating goals they can realistically achieve in the short term while dreaming big for the long term, they create a path for themselves.

This makes decision-making very easy for them because their goals inform them about how they need to proceed. Should they change roles? Should they seek another job? While these questions prompt thought, the action they take is never indecisive because it is in line with their goals at all times.

Dream

I mentioned that goals need to be realistic in the short term and dreamy in the long term in the previous point. So how and why should you do this? Well, this approach combines the power of both sets of advice when it comes to goal setting. If you set goals that are unrealistic in the short term, your self-image is going to take a blow and will let you know well in advance that what you're doing is pointless.

However, over the long term, human beings are perfectly terrible at prediction. The long-term results of any task are an exponential function of all the actions that go into creating it. In plain English, there's a lot of stuff that goes into a long-term result, and you can't predict how much of an effect one portion will have over another. They always add up to a sum greater than the parts.

Hence, dreaming big and writing it down is a great way to motivate yourself and give direction to your career and life. You'll find that all confident people practice this in one form or another. Break down that big unrealistic goal into smaller goals and get more realistic the smaller the time frame is. You'll find that you'll end up creating a perfect career path.

Network

In order to be successful in their careers, confident people realize the value of networking. Even if they are introverted, they understand that, ultimately, you are your Rolodex. Even in jobs that are socially isolated, like many in the financial sector are, they understand that building a network is an insurance policy against tough times that will inevitably come.

Isn't this a pessimistic outlook? Well, not quite. I'll explain this train of thought in more detail in Chapter 6. For now, understand that tough times will come, and you need insurance for them. The great thing is that networking becomes easier the more you do it, and people report higher levels of confidence the more they practice it.

Make Time

Confident people don't necessarily love what they do for work. That's a bit of a shock, isn't it? Isn't passion necessary for work satisfaction? Aren't we all supposed to be a bunch of happy little daisies in a fresh field basking in the warm sunshine? Not quite. Life isn't as clear-cut as that.

The most misunderstood piece of advice is the whole 'follow your passion' movement. This book is not about all of that, so I'm just going to say that you need to indulge in what's important to you, but this doesn't mean you need to quit your job. Confident people make time to do what they really love doing.

Whether it's tinkering with motorcycles or building a time machine on the side, they adopt a practical view of things and are thankful for the good things their career gives them, even if it isn't their dream job.

Eliminate

Negativity and negative people. Every confident person has either minimized or eliminated these two things from their lives, and it's no different in the workplace. You will not find career high fliers gossiping about people behind their backs or standing around complaining about how their boss is a mutton-headed oaf.

As a matter of fact, you're unlikely to even find them complaining about work because they understand that work is what pays for their leisure time. I'm not saying they walk around with smiles plastered on their faces all the time but they view things in perspective.

Eliminate the negativity in your job and you'll be surprised at how much easier work becomes and how much more effective you are at what you do. Structuring your work life around these principles is what achieves such a result.

Social Confidence

This is a big one. We all want to be that person who walks in and gets the whole room to look at them in stunned silence. Well, I've got news for you. You're probably mistaking popularity for confidence if that's your idea of social confidence. The reason social confidence is often so elusive is that people build up unrealistic expectations of how they ought to appear.

So this section is as much about showing you what it looks like as much as it is about readjusting your expectations.

Feel Good

Confidence flows from how you feel about yourself. Socially confident people feel attractive, and this begins with taking care of themselves and wearing clothes they feel attractive in. Why is the little black dress such a popular dress item for women? Well, because it makes you feel attractive. It makes you feel good.

The truth is that people will often treat you the way you tell them to treat you. If you turn up shoddily dressed and looking like you just rolled out of bed, you're not giving anyone a reason to respect you. I mean, you don't value yourself so why should they value you?

Dress well and learn how to groom yourself. This goes a long way in making you confident, not just in social settings but in every setting. Lounge about in your jammie jams in your home and around loved ones but outside and around people who don't know you, put your best foot forward.

Listen

Socially savvy people know when to listen and when to shut up. Is there some secret skill in knowing when to listen? Not really. It begins by taking a genuine interest in the person who is talking to you. You needn't try to figure out what their grandma's favorite dessert was, but at a minimum, pay attention to the topic and take an active interest in what they're saying. Can you contribute something of use to the conversation?

If yes, speak up. If not, shut up. Every confident person follows this simple rule. It begins with sincerity. If you go into conversations with the intention of forcing yourself into things, you only come across as annoying. The only exception to this rule is when you've earned the trust of the group and the people in it know you well.

In such cases, you can get away with being a bit annoying. In most social situations, this is the type of interaction you will actually see where older members of the group display arrogance and everyone goes along with it. Someone who is looking to model this starts equating arrogance with confidence and ends up aggravating everyone.

So what if you're genuinely not interested in what the other person is saying? Well, you're in the wrong group! Seek out people who are interesting to you. It's a big world, after all.

Responsibility

This is something a confident person does as a part of their life in every situation. Taking responsibility is a huge indicator of confidence because you're admitting that yes you can mess up and no you're not ashamed of it, as long as you tried your best. Do not mistake this for excessive self-deprecation.

Confident people own up to their mistakes but don't overly apologize for them. They apologize once and then move on and try to rectify their mistake. An insecure person, in contrast, is constantly apologizing and is constantly putting themselves down. This doesn't mean confident people never make fun of themselves; it's just that it doesn't happen excessively.

Striking a balance is all about understanding the secret to charisma. Charismatic people are ideals of confidence, and emulating them is a great way to build confidence in yourself. So what is the secret to charisma?

Well, it's not what you might be thinking of.

Unlock Charisma

Charisma is something that many people have tried to decode over the years. However, in my opinion, it is the best-selling author and thinker Mark Manson who hit the nail on the head when he pronounced that the true secret to confidence, charisma, and even success is vulnerability. When he made this statement, it caused a lot of confusion understandably.

Look back over all of the qualities we've run through thus far when taking a look at confident people's behaviors in different situations or contexts. When it comes to money, what is something confident people do? They don't hesitate to ask for help.

Socially confident people own up to their mistakes and don't hesitate to shut up when they have nothing of value to add. Which quality are they displaying? In a word, vulnerability.

You'll see that charismatic leaders everywhere, the truly charismatic ones, display vulnerability openly. Admitting your flaws openly is the most powerful statement of confidence there is. Telling everyone that this is who they are and that they're okay with it is a powerful endorsement of the fact that they believe in themselves.

Charismatic people are vulnerable but not weak. Owning up to and displaying vulnerability is a show of strength. Not the Genghis Khan type of martial strength but a more grounded, balanced, and human strength. There is a difference between true strength and displays of it.

Examining world leaders gives us examples of both. Setting aside politics, let's evaluate some of them through the lens of vulnerability. The most obvious case study is Donald Trump.

He is anything but vulnerable. Yet, his fan base finds him charismatic. Is this because he really is charismatic or is he ticking the boxes they want to see? How long will this impression last? Well, frankly, I don't know.

The fact is that Trump displays many genuine qualities of confident people in his behavior. However, his popular persona is not something to model your confidence after because like every politician, he's playing a role. Examining his actions will provide a better explanation of his good qualities and bad. Having the confidence to rebound and build his wealth after making colossal mistakes is a sign of huge confidence when it comes to money. Understanding how to sell a narrative is a sign of massive confidence in his own abilities to understand his market.

Flexing his muscles on Twitter and calling people 'rocket boy' or 'crooked Hillary' isn't. Labeling himself a 'stable genius' isn't. Learning to differentiate between what is an act and what is true confidence is made easier by looking at actions through the lens of vulnerability.

Model those behaviors that come from a vulnerable intent and you'll find terrific role models in people, whether you agree with their politics or not.

This brings to an end the theory section of this book. From now on, we're going to be all about practice and action. The following chapters are going to give you both everyday exercises as well as deep tools to reprogram your mind for massive confidence.

When practicing them, keep in mind everything you've learned about thus far and remember the importance of vulnerability. More than anything else, let this inform your intention, and everything else will flow from it. If you're still unclear about the concept of vulnerability, I highly recommend reading Mark Manson's website (you'll find this in the references section) or his best-selling books.

Chapter 5: First Steps to Building Confidence

So your intention is in the right place. You want to build your confidence and self-esteem, either in all areas of your life or in particular situations. Great, what's next? This chapter and the rest of this book are going to show you exactly how you can do this in your life.

The exercises and actions you will learn about will start with simple mental attitudes and progress to more complex ones involving visualization. There is a reason for this scaling. You see, your brain is in a comfort zone right now and has built a lot of habits that undermine your self-esteem.

If you were to jump in and try to move yourself far outside of your comfort zone, your brain would rebel and drag you right back in. Cue disappointment and further reinforcement of a negative self-image. The thing to do is to work your way forward, slowly and steadily. This way you'll be pushing the limits but in a way that will allow you to combat the inevitable pushback your brain is going to give you.

The exercises in this chapter are aimed at getting your brain used to your new habits. Some of them might not make sense intuitively, but they work. The key is to practice them every day, bit by bit. I wish there was a key I could give you that would unlock instant charisma, but this isn't possible biologically as you've seen.

Repetition is essential, so commit to this program. With that being said, let's jump into the first technique.

Create Mental States

If you suffer from a lack of confidence, there have probably been times when you have stumbled into a state of mind where you felt invincible. This might have been brought about by some external stimulus, but the lesson here is that your confidence is really just a state of mind.

You might also have noticed that these confident states vanish far too quickly and reaching out for them causes a lot of frustration. They feel really good and you want them back, but the more you reach for them, the further away from them you end up.

Stop reaching for things and instead move forward slowly and steadily. As you go about your day, adopt the following mental states with regard to everything that happens in your life.

Solution-Oriented Mindset

This is an extremely simple technique but will do wonders for you. The premise is simple: Whenever things go wrong in your life, from your toast burning to you losing your job, adopt a solution-oriented mindset. This means relentlessly seek solutions at all times.

At first, this is going to be tough. When a problem hits, your brain is going to spiral out of control and you're going to start imagining all sorts of nightmarish scenarios. No matter how hard you try to wrench its focus back to a solution, it will refuse to respond.

Here's the thing: The success or failure of this technique lies not in whether you could focus on the solution. It depends entirely upon whether you made the effort or not. So keep making the effort, and don't worry about what the outcome is. If you just embarrassed yourself in front of a group of strangers, focus on the solution. Yes, your brain is going to start running away with itself, but what is a possible solution to the current problem?

Focus on doing that. Whenever your brain brings up an image that paints a picture of a problem, ask yourself, what can I do? Keep doing this, and your brain will get the message and start automatically doing it without your prompting. Becoming a solution oriented person will change your life, instead of stewing in problems you immediately move into problem solving action.

Their Puppy Just Died

When you have low confidence, you'll find that people will treat you differently. They'll probably place unfair labels on you. This problem is compounded if your regular expression happens to coincide with a level of tension in your face. People will likely think of you as being short-tempered or angry all the time. Well, you can't change what they think of you no matter how unfair their judgments are. What you can change is your outlook toward them.

So, with this in mind, here's the solution: Treat and talk to everyone who judges you unfairly as if their puppy died that morning. Adopt this view with everyone who offends you or angers you. Their puppy just died. That sweet, innocent, frolicking little bundle of joy tragically passed away, and they're extremely cut up about it, as you can imagine.

The beauty of adopting this mental state is that not only does it restrain you from upsetting yourself, but it also projects an attitude of confidence that people will pick up on. Think back to a time when you witnessed someone being completely unflappable in the face of harsh treatment.

You may have witnessed a few traffic accidents in your life. Well, think of the usual fender benders where people get into arguments. Who is the more confident person? The guy screaming at the top of his lungs acting out on his road rage or the other guy who's calm and rational? The answer is obvious.

Don't allow your mood and your mental state to be hijacked by those inferior to you. Remain calm and be yourself at all times. Use this trick to adopt a pitiful and compassionate view of the other person, and you'll find that people will view you in a different light, little by little.

Fail at Something New Every Day

Every morning you wake up, rub your hand with glee and ask yourself 'so what should I fail at today?' This is one of the more counter-intuitive methods of thinking that will increase your confidence. You need not follow the gleeful portion of the first sentence, but you get what I mean. Try something new every day and see if you can fail at it.

At this point, I should point out that you need to exercise your common sense. This doesn't mean you walk up to a stranger, insult them, and see if you can get away with it without being punched in the face.

Anyway, the point of this exercise is to push the limits of your skills and comfort zone. Say you've wanted to do something but haven't had the courage to, at least try even if there will be some type of failure along the way.

Here's your chance! See if you can fail at it! If you're worried that people will make fun of you or look at your weird, let them do so. This just means you failed at it pushed your limits and achieved your task.

Try to deliberately push yourself to the point of failure, only this way can you find your limitations.

This is an attitude you need to adopt, not a task with a definite goal. If you find yourself contemplating an action but find that you lack the confidence to carry it out, tell yourself 'well, let me see if I can fail at it!'

Aim for something to fail at every day. This only applies to new stuff and not at the things you have already mastered. So if you're an ace programmer, writing a bad piece of code that day doesn't count. It has to be something you've felt uncomfortable about or have felt some apprehension about the activity.

Be Optimistic, Then Pessimistic

I have a problem with constant optimism. You may not have picked up on it in the previous chapter, but I think extreme optimism as a strategy is severely overrated. Life doesn't obey your optimism or pessimism. There are times when you will stare failure right in the face and know that you fully deserve it because you haven't been giving your best.

Carl Zimmerman

Pasting a smile onto your face and saying 'all is well' in such situations is like going to sleep in the middle of a burning house. It's just ridiculous. Pessimism has its advantages, and you need to use it wisely. The issue is that you've probably been using optimism and pessimism the wrong way around all this while, and you've wired yourself the wrong way round.

So, here's what you do: When contemplating the thought of starting a new task, be a realist, not an optimist or a pessimist.

Pessimism is the critic; it can be very powerful because it helps ensure that you double-check the details. If you have a speech prepared, expect to deliver it well as you're writing it or planning its structure. Once this is done, think of what would happen if you stumbled or had the audience gasp in shock at something inappropriate you just said. Go over your speech again and check to see if there's something you've screwed up in there.

You have some pessimism and maybe even imagined being embarrassed in front of all those people, you still have doubts, its ok its, natural to feel this way.

Keep practicing until the activity becomes boring, you could do it backwards. You will probably hate the speech by now, just because you have heard it so much. Keep practicing boredom is no reason to stop, it's just an indicator that you are mastering the practice.

With better preparation comes confidence. You'll find that your brain will agree that you've done your best and the stress will lower. Whatever happens now will happen.

Body Language

In 2012, social psychologist and associate professor at Harvard Business School Amy Cuddy delivered a TED talk that has become one of the most cited on the subject of body language and confidence. In her talk, Cuddy expanded on a number of principles that were illuminating. Although her talk was aimed at salespeople, there are a number of lessons for you to adopt from it.

The funny thing is that you already know a lot of this stuff. After all, your mom most likely told you about this when you were a kid.

Eye Contact

People who lack social confidence, be it in any situation, tend to fumble this one the most. You have those who keep staring at people in the eye all the time and those who steadfastly refuse to look others in the eye. If you're a man, the former practice is likely to land you in a fight with another man. If you're a woman, you'll just be seen as being too high strung.

As for avoiding eye contact, both sexes will be seen as being too meek if they do this. Proper eye contact is an art and a science. If you find looking into another person's eyes intimidating, there are some easy solutions for you to adopt. Instead of staring right at their irises, look at their nose instead. Don't go all the way to the tip but stay somewhere between the bridge of their nose and the tip. Unless you happen to be really close to someone, they're unlikely to be able to tell the difference.

When you do this, practice darting your eyes back up into their eyes and then move back to their nose. This sort of eye movement is reassuring for the other person since it mimics how people normally behave when they're engaged. Now, my intention isn't to give you a trick to fake engagement. Listen to what they have to say in a genuine manner.

Except for a very small number of situations, it is always better to excuse yourself from an uninteresting situation rather than fake engagement.

Posture

Don't slouch, shoulders back, chin up, and chest out! Everyone has received this lesson in one form or another. This posture not only projects confidence but actually is a healthy one. Your airways are not blocked when you stand like this and you'll end up breathing properly.

Weight distribution plays an important role when standing up. Face the person you're speaking to and place your feet shoulder-width apart and maintain equal weight distribution between both feet. Have your hands resting by the side and maintain eye contact as described previously.

When meeting someone for the first time, especially in a context other than work, don't turn your body toward them completely. Instead, maintain an angle of 45 degrees when speaking to them. This is especially applicable to men meeting people who are physically smaller than them. It can be intimidating to have a bigger person turn themselves entirely to you so open yourself toward them slowly.

When sitting on a chair, practice good posture. Keep your spine straight and feet planted the floor firmly. This strengthens your core and keeps your body prepared to maintain good posture when standing as well. If you're struggling to figure out what a good posture is, stand up against a wall and keep your spine straight.

You'll notice that your rear, the back of your head, and the back of your shoulders touch the wall. This is a power posture you want to adopt.

Fidgeting

Some people have trouble controlling their hands. They tend to get excited and start waving them around all over the place, like a traffic cop. Some amount of waving is necessary in a normal interaction but do too much of it and people will stop paying attention to your words and will stare at your hands instead.

If you have this problem, it's a good idea to weigh your hands down with something when talking. Hold a book or a glass when talking to someone. Don't hold a pen or something pointy since you'll end up poking someone's eye out.

Women who like playing around with their hair or shifting their weight onto either foot when talking are victims of fidgeting as well. In some romantic situations, this works well, but in a business setting you'll end up looking like a ditz. So consciously avoid doing these things and weigh your hands down. Jamming your hands into your pockets is also to be avoided.

General advice is to not fold your arms in front of a person when they're talking to you. This is good advice, but it can be awkward to stand there with your arms hanging by your side when talking to someone. What you can do is instead of crossing your arms, place one hand on your chin while resting that arm's elbow on the palm of the other.

This projects an attitude of interest in what the other person is saying and shows engagement. In case you're nodding off to sleep, it provides excellent support and prevents you from nodding off.

Walking and Handshakes

A basic principle of body language to apply to your walking is to keep your chin up. Some people have problems with this because they don't know what to look at. Well, look into the horizon at nothing in particular. It takes some adjustment, but keeping your chin up and chest out while walking will actually help you feel more energized and will aid your mental states.

When walking, aim to take longer strides than you normally do. You will feel like an ostrich at first but aim for something slightly longer than usual. Also, slow your movement down. People low on confidence tend to take short, hurried steps. Make your pacing more deliberate and reduce the speed of your actions. I'm not saying you need to move in slow motion but to reduce your actions by a beat.

This conveys to your brain that things are fine and you will stop engaging your fast brain and involve your slow, rational brain more. This will lead to more consideration before your decisions, and you'll end up making better ones. This won't happen overnight but with time, you'll see the benefits.

Handshakes are another hot zone of confidence. Here is another place where people take things too far, especially men. Every sales interview is a competition to see who can crush the interviewer's hand the hardest, and some morons take a lot of pride in their vice-like grip and purposely aim to crush the other person's hand. Don't be this person.

Instead, give the other person's hand a squeeze and a single shake. Don't overdo it beyond this. If you want extra credit, try this as well. If your hand gets crushed by the other person, call them out on it by telling them to ease up on the grip in a playful manner.

An important point to remember when shaking the other person's hand is to grip the portion of their hand just below the fingers where the palm starts, with your thumb and forefinger. Don't grip their fingers since this doesn't feel very pleasant. This happens a lot when men shake women's hands which are smaller. The woman's hand tends to be gobbled up and her fingers get squeezed. So take care with this.

Practice your handshake with a friend or by turning your left hand with its thumb down and grip your right hand. It might not be perfect but it should give you an idea of where to grip another person's hand.

Speaking and Listening

Speaking in public tends to give the strongest of people the jitters but of far more importance is to speak confidently in close quarters. This sort of speaking is where people form impressions of you and is the sort of talking you'll be doing most of the time. A key tool to speak well is to first listen with attention and intent.

People tend to focus too much on the speaking and ignore the listening. This is true of both confident people and those who struggle with it. We're in too much of a hurry to have a chance to speak instead of actually listening to what is being communicated. There's a thin line between confidence and arrogance, and listening is it.

People who are not confident unfortunately model arrogant people since this sort of behavior is more prevalent. Use the tips in this section to figure out the difference and land on the right side all the time.

Modulation and Tonality

Men, encourage that deep bass in your voice. Women, stop talking like a small child in order to get attention. These tips alone will do wonders for how people treat you, and in turn, this will increase your confidence. Another thing to practice is voice modulation and tonality. Modulation refers to the pitch of your voice and tonality is simply the tone (duh).

Let's start with tonality and American presidents are great examples of this. Barack Obama's tone was largely one of respectful consideration, whereas Donald Trump's tone is mostly dismissive. Them illustrate different types of confidence, but Trump tends to violate the line of arrogance to the point of obliteration.

Study tapes of both men and you'll see how their tonality shifts depending on how sure they are of themselves. Obama tended to belt his words out faster while Trump dials up the dismissiveness a notch. My point is that tonality communicates a lot about what you're thinking, and people pick up on this quite easily.

So what does a confident tone sound like? Well, you want to sound respectful but firm and Obama, Bill Clinton, and Ronald Reagan are good examples of this. The former British Prime Minister Winston Churchill, despite being a revered leader, was someone who crossed into arrogance quite a lot. Perhaps this is because most of his examples come from wartime speeches, in which case such posturing is understandable.

Your tonality is linked to how well you can modulate your voice. People low on confidence tend to have low pitches and a monotone voice. If you've ever learned a foreign language, think back to what your voice sounded like when you were learning to speak sentences. Your voice probably ended on a higher pitch than when it started and it was monotone.

Ending a sentence with a higher pitch is the vocal equivalent of a question mark at the end of it. If you're stating a fact this doesn't make you sound very confident, as you can imagine. Actors are great models when it comes to studying voice modulation. After all, this is a part of their training.

When studying, it helps to look at the extreme examples, and when it comes to voice modulation, there is no more extreme example of the British Shakespearean stage actor, Brian Blessed. You've probably not heard of Blessed, and your life is poorer for it. YouTube is littered with videos of him appearing on comedy shows, and I'm not going to ruin the fun you're going to have by describing what you'll see.

Another good example of how voice modulation can completely change a person's character is to study the English actor Hugh Laurie. You might know him as Doctor House from the TV series of the same name. In case you didn't know that Laurie was British, you might have been astounded to learn this fact. Even more astounding is that Laurie is actually known more for his comedy back in England than drama.

Contrast Dr. House with Laurie's portrayals of Bertie Wooster in *Jeeves and Wooster* and his portrayals of Lt. George, Prince George IV, and Prince Ludwig the Indestwuctible (not a typo) on *Blackadder* and you'll see how voice modulation turns a great comedian into a two-time Golden Globe winner for his lead role in dramas.

Carl Zimmerman

This section is heavy on examples because voices are better heard than explained. Just remember to flex your voice up and down and do not sound arrogant when you speak. A side tip to sound confident is to make statements in place of questions. So instead of asking someone 'where are you from?' say 'you're from Alaska, aren't you?' This will lead them to ask you why you think they're from Alaska and a conversation will flow from there.

Speaking of conversations...

Learn How to Talk

Banter is the lifeblood of any good conversation. When you first meet someone, there isn't much to talk about, but you need to talk anyway. This is even more true if you're the one who's approached the other person, as guys in singles bars have found out to their dismay over the years.

Now, I'll confess, banter is meaningless jabbering for the most part, and it is tiresome. Do not make the mistake of thinking it is useless, though. If you think it's useless, you just can't see the meaning in it that others can. Banter is just a way of getting people comfortable with one another before you can move onto more serious topics. Constant banter is what is wasteful; introductory banter is the opposite.

So how do you run your mouth? Well, you need to develop a feel for these things since so much of it is organic. Making statements instead of questions is a great way to project confidence and get the other person talking. A good thing to do is to prepare a list of four or five topics to riff about beforehand.

Making statements about the other person being from a particular place is a good go-to topic. Another good topic to talk about is the place you find yourself in. You can mention how you've been here before and how it reminds you of this other place and so on. A good way of practicing your ability to riff on anything is to pick a subject and then talk about it for two minutes straight.

You'll find that you'll actually need only two or three at the most in order to get the person to feel comfortable around you.

Asking other people in the group about their opinion of something is another great hack to appear in charge without doing much talking.

When someone directs a question toward you and you don't have a clue what to say, don't be afraid to say you do not understand or have little knowledge of the topic. You can't hold yourself to the impossible standard of being able to speak on every subject.

So, listen with sincerity and if you can't understand something, ask people to explain further and show genuine interest.

Learn to Listen

This isn't going to be a long section since listening is simple. The reason you might be thinking of it as being hard is that you're either not sincerely interested in what the other person is saying and thus, you cannot differentiate the difference between hearing and listening.

Most people wait for their turn to talk instead of listening and frankly, there's no hack for this or some solution. You need to approach every interaction with the intention to listen. If you find it difficult to muster this intention, you're probably hanging out with the wrong sort of people, and you need to change your environment.

You should try to place equal value on listening and speaking, you can learn from both but your more likely to learn from listening.

A key to good listening is to be aware of your own biases when doing so. We are susceptible to all sorts of biases, from the confirmation bias to a bias for blondes over brunettes. So, ask yourself if you're reacting to the other person's words out of some ingrained bias.

Simply striving to be as objective as you can while listening will place you ahead of most people. Your lack of ambition to judge the other person and shut down their ideas should increase the quality of your interactions.

Always ask questions and probe for more meaning in what the other person has just said. This usually comes automatically when you're honestly listening to someone.

Having the expectation that other people have valuable insights and information hidden away inside them, should give you all the motivation you need to be a better listener.

Carl Zimmerman

Chapter 6: Exercises to Calm Your Mind

In this chapter, we're going to dive deeper and change things from the inside. Your mind is what determines your view of the world, and the key to developing long-term confidence is to train it to view things in a less uncertain manner.

This is the real issue you face. Your confidence is low because of the incorrect expectations you're placing on things in your life. Adjust your expectations and you'll find that coping with situations becomes a lot easier. Seemingly negative situations can turn into victories. It's all about your point of view and what you do with it.

Prepare your mind every day with these methods, and you'll see that everything that was highlighted in the previous chapter will come automatically to you. Confidence is about removing the layers of bad information and revealing your true self.

Stoic Acceptance

It's become pretty chic to be stoic these days, and is followed by CEO's, sport start teams and many people living high performance life styles.

Stoic philosophy was born out of an amalgamation of a number of other philosophies and is best thought of as a set of principles to live one's life by. Unlike many philosophies that can be impractical, Stoicism is mainly concerned with facing reality and priming your expectations of what life throws at you.

The result is a set of principles that will serve you wonderfully well through both good times and bad.

You don't need to follow every single tenet of Stoicism in order to reap its rewards. The following sections discuss the best Stoic principles to follow in your life and build confidence in yourself.

Amor Fati

This translates literally to 'a love of fate.' A lot of life is random, and you don't really have control over many things. The problem with human beings is that we overestimate our ability to influence results when really, there isn't much we can do about them. This is a deflating thought on the surface, but dig deeper and you'll find that it is extremely empowering.

Stoicism proposes that human beings should focus on controlling only that which they can control. This means you focus on your actions and your thoughts.

By controlling yourself, you prepare yourself better to face the world. Amor fati is an extension of this view in that it recommends you love your life as it is. Whatever fate may bring.

Stoicism gets you to adopt an objective rational view of your life and also gets you to start taking responsibility for it.

Control whatever you can control and leave the rest to fate. You can't control your fate, so you might as well love it. Love might be a strong word, as far as I can tell the word is used like an unconditional acceptance of reality. Reality as it is, not as you want it to be.

Human beings are a part of nature and everything in this world originates from the same thing, and we will fade away like all things in the natural world. This is the reality of things and no matter how hard you try to fight it mentally; it will not work.

Accept the fact you are part of a natural process, life and death. We live in a world full of imperfection, this is the way it is and always will be. Amor Fati

Take responsibility and love the best you can, no matter what happens. It's all you have.

Action. Not Thinking

The Stoics placed huge importance on the fact that a person needs to go out there and practice this stuff. It isn't enough for you to sit there and wonder about how everything is connected and so on. You need to put this stuff into practice and see how it goes for yourself.

Controlling what you can control is a central tenet of Stoic thought, and in this context, it means that you need to think of the future while making your plans and then get into journey mode. Forget about the end result and instead focus on executing the next step. The result will take care of itself. Amor fati.

Taking action immerses you in the things you wish to manifest in your life, and this is what produces results. Become a doer and take steps toward your chosen goals. A person who has direction is always confident.

Expect the Worst

This is the most misunderstood tenet of Stoic philosophy. Seneca, one of the three great Stoic philosophers, is famous for writing that a person ought to always expect the worst in everything that they do. Due to the vagaries of translation, modern English doesn't quite capture what this thought process is all about, so let's look at it further.

Seneca means to say that when carrying out a task, have no expectations or low expectations. Plan ahead and execute to the best of your abilities but recognize that the result is out of your hands. The Stoics placed a high value on virtue as being the ultimate goal of a human being's life.

Virtue lies in executing the process and controlling what you can control. The results you achieve, whether it be a success or failure, are something outside of you and the Stoics classified this as 'indifferents.' Some indifferents like success are preferred and some are dispreferred.

It doesn't change the fact that it is still an indifferent. It is perfectly acceptable to chase an indifferent (success), but a person ought to remember that virtue is the highest goal, not the indifferent. This means you need to divorce yourself from the result and focus on the process that needs to be executed.

Having no expectations removes the emotional attachment you have, and it is this emotional attachment that causes confidence problems in the first place. You worry and fret about achieving something and don't want to screw it up. You're worried people will laugh at you when you deliver your speech.

Well, whether they laugh or not, what is the virtue inherent in this situation? You need to deliver a good speech on the topic, preferably one from which people will learn something and gain some type of value. So prepare a good speech and practice reciting it. Practice your tonality and adopt power poses as discussed in the previous chapter. Do all of this, try your best and the result takes care of itself.

Plato's View

Plato was not a Stoic but some of his views make it into the teachings of Euripides, whose words, in turn, are echoed by Marcus Aurelius, who was one of the last competent emperors of the Western Roman empire. Plato spoke at great length about recognizing one's own mortality and of adopting a view that was far above the one currently prevailing.

If you have a problem right now and cannot figure out how to approach your boss and ask them for a raise, ask yourself how much does this moment really matter in the grand scheme of things?

Now, visualize the entire building. Then the entire block, postal code, city, country, continent, planet, solar system, galaxy, and so on. What does your petty little issue really amount to? The world will keep moving on and you yourself will likely forget it within a few hours.

Marcus was a huge proponent of adopting Plato's view, and this was a guy who ran Rome, the pre-eminent power in the world. As such, he was the most powerful man in the world in his time, he dealt with so much weight on his shoulders it's impossible for us to even imagine, and it worked for him. Odds are it's going to work for you as well.

Physical Practices

Carl Zimmerman

Your mind and body are linked and the better shape your body is in, the more alert and fresh your mind is. Research showing the benefits of exercising is well-known, to the point that everyone agrees its beneficial. Anyway, here are some of the benefits:

- More energy
- More clarity
- Better quality of life
- Lesser healthcare costs

More of all the good stuff and less of the bad stuff. A lack of confidence is often a result of poor physical shape. You don't need to look like a supermodel, just fix your diet and workout. Aim to get healthy instead of 'in shape.' The ideal shape varies from generation to generation.

There was a time when runway models were supposed to be stick thin. These days, models who are ridiculously thin are actually bullied. So stop trying to fit into someone else's standards and aim for health and well-being.

Exercise

So how much do you need to exercise and which workout regime should you follow? If you've never exercised before, just do something. It doesn't matter if it's a schedule to go walk in your neighborhood park every day for an hour, just do something. If you used to work out and have fallen out of the habit, getting fit is a lot easier since you've had a taste of it before.

Everyone—and this includes women—needs to focus on building strength in one form or another. Whether you choose to do this by joining a gym or just lifting heavy bags all day, you need to build muscle. Strength training has been shown to provide far more long-term benefits than just cardio.

More importantly, strength training is going to challenge you mentally like no other workout can. The best part is that most strength workouts last only from forty-five minutes to an hour. The bad news is that there's a reason they're so short. You'll be working at a very high intensity, and you're going to be exhausted from it.

However, this is a good exhaustion, if that makes any sense. You'll feel a sense of accomplishment when you finish your workout, and when you begin to notice the muscle growth in your mirror around the three-month mark, trust me, you'll run out and sign up for more workouts.

There are two major beginner strength training programs out there, Starting Strength and Stronglifts 5X5. Both of them contain the same exercises and are pretty similar. Both require you to work out three to four days per week, so overall, you'll be working in the gym for around four hours per week at the most. This really isn't much of a time commitment when looked at this way.

Women have a mental block when it comes to strength training thanks to mainstream stereotyping of women who work out as being too masculine. This is nonsense. No woman will ever look like a man just because she starts lifting some weight. So get over your embarrassment and lift like a man does.

If you love some other form of physical activity like swimming or running, I'd still recommend strength training. This is because you'll perform better at those activities the stronger you are. At this point, you're probably wondering where you're going to find the motivation from.

Well, what can I say? Your physical presence and the image looking back at you in the mirror gives most people a confidence boost. A precise physical goal to push towards is a great motivator.

The best way to maintain discipline is to create a routine you enjoy that you can perform with your eyes closed. If you make things too difficult you will struggle to maintain your routine, and you're likely to drop it at the first sign of trouble.

People think that their willpower will get them over the hurdle, but the truth is that willpower can be depleted when energy is at a low level.

Try not to exhaust yourself and end up worse off than before. Always do things in a way that makes things easy so you want to come back. For example, if you find it difficult to get up early in the morning and workout then, don't do it. Stop trying to will yourself to get up early if it makes you miserable. Make a more suitable time for yourself instead.

Nutrition

More than the amount of time you spend working out, your nutrition is what is going to affect your health. These days it's very easy to obtain fast food and even healthy-looking fast food. With all due respect to the avocado smoothie joint down the road, the healthiest food is the stuff you cook at home that is made with fresh natural ingredients.

It's a reflection of the sorry state of the food industry that we even have a category called whole food, instead of just calling it food. This is food as close to its natural form as possible. I'm not trying to say you should eat everything raw, just that you should avoid the stuff that has a high number of chemical additives or preservatives in it.

Things like TV dinners, frozen food (unless the food is in its natural form), and so on are full of chemicals and sugar that stop it from getting spoiled. As you can imagine, none of these things are good for your body. Sugar is what causes you to get fat, not healthy fat like butter or cream eaten in excess.

The majority of American food contains far too much sugar and too little protein. So focus on using natural ingredients, organic when possible, and learn how to cook them. You don't need to follow any fancy diet. Just eat when hungry and aim to eat until you're 80% full.

Listen to your body and feed it when you need to and you'll be just fine. Avoid refined or processed foods and use naturally grown produce and meat in your diet, and you'll automatically become healthy(unless you have a food allergy). Aim to eat a balanced diet that meets your nutritional needs and you'll avoid a lot of the lethargy that is caused by imbalanced diets.

A balanced diet is easier to eat than most people think. Simply eat a little bit of everything that is untouched by chemicals or cooking methods that induce them. Sure, you can still eat some junk food now and then, but the majority of your diet should be whole food.

Limit your intake of sugar, caffeine, and alcohol, and you'll develop a healthy relationship with your food.

Meditation

That meditation is a way to calm your mind should come as no surprise. Whatever you think of ancient Eastern philosophy, there is no denying that some of its practices make a lot of sense for all of us.

Almost every form of Buddhist meditation is non-religious in nature and carries simple techniques.

In case you've been living under a rock, you might be wondering what the big deal about meditation is. Well, meditation literally changes your brain function for the better. There are different techniques you can use to build different attributes, but the main Buddhist techniques involve the development of awareness and focus.

Meditation ultimately aims to enable you to let go of your ego and its constant need for validation. Your lack of confidence really stems from this portion of your mind. All of us develop an ego as we grow older, and thanks to its relentless need for emotional fuel, the ego ends up creating situations that are exaggerated. This, in turn, creates either overconfidence or a lack of it.

A lack of balance is the hallmark of the ego. If you find yourself leaning too far toward a particular opinion on anything, you're likely acting out of the ego and are projecting either your own insecurities or imperfect understanding onto something. Politics is currently mired in such dualistic thinking.

The reality is that a lot of that stuff is not going to affect you in the least so you're better off simply turning away from it and focusing on yourself. As mentioned earlier, there are two main purposes of Buddhist meditation at the basic levels: awareness and focus. Let's look at these one-by-one.

Awareness

Meditation to build awareness starts with your breath. To begin, relax your body and either sit on the floor in the lotus position or sit upright in a chair. Keep your eyes open as you begin to take deep breaths. As you inhale, notice how your body tenses up, and as you exhale, notice how all of that tension can be let go.

Become more aware of your body and your environment by noticing any sounds nearby and any ambient noise that exists. Now, slowly close your eyes and being counting your breath. Count once for every inhalation and once for every exhalation. When you reach five, reset your count back to one.

As you count, you'll notice that your mind will want to run away somewhere else to another thought. This is perfectly normal, and once you realize your mind has run away, gently bring your awareness and attention back to your breath and resume counting. Don't expect your mind to be able to concentrate deeply on your breath. Instead, focus on your breath count as much as possible and keep bringing your awareness to your breath every time your attention turns away from it.

Carry out this exercise for at least five minutes daily. Once you're used to practicing it, you can turn things up a notch by letting go of the count and simply observing your breath. Notice qualities about your breath such as how hot it feels or how cool it is. Which nostril do your inhale and exhale come from and where below your nose does your breath hit once you exhale and so on?

This is a little more difficult since you do not have a count anchoring you in place, but it creates a higher level of awareness with regard to what your mind is doing. You'll notice a distinct moment between when a stimulus arises and your mind's desire to chase it. It is in delaying this and eventually ignoring this want of your mind that change occurs.

As a further practice, you can then leave your breath and scan your body from top to bottom. Notice any sensations that occur and keep traveling within your body top to bottom and from the bottom to the top. Scan every portion of yourself for sensations you feel and remain equanimous to all of it.

If something is hurting, simply observe it and move on. Do not make any effort to alleviate the problem. This is easier said than done, but over time, you'll begin to see that the pain dissolves away. All you'll be left with is a sense of vibration. Mind you this doesn't come overnight and takes years to build up to.

Either way, observing yourself when sitting still is the hardest thing to do, and this practice will build discipline and will also build awareness with regard to how your mind works and rushes from pillar to post most of the time.

You can start meditating by downloading the Headspace app or even better, search for a retreat near you where you can learn from a qualified instructor. Mind you these retreats are not a vacation and are hard work. So make sure you understand what it is you're signing up for before heading off to one.

Focus

Meditation to build focus follows a slightly different path. In this, you don't develop an awareness within as much as focus on something on the outside. The first step to take is to count your breath as mentioned in the previous section, but instead of stopping at five, go all the way to twenty and back.

If you notice along the way that your mind is distracted even a little bit, reset the count. This is challenging at first since most people will unknowingly make it to twenty and think they've achieved some sort of prize. The truth is that most people will struggle to make it past three. It's just that beginners are unaware of what their mind is focusing on for the most part.

After a week of counting in this manner, it's time to focus on a single point in front of you. Simply focus your gaze on this point and do not count or do anything else. Notice simultaneously how your mind yearns to break free and how you need to struggle to keep it in place. At some point, you'll find that it is a lot easier to let your mind wander than it is to focus on the point.

Don't fight your mind and instead look to work with it gently. After a week of focusing on a point, light a candle and begin focusing on the dark portion on the flame, which is closest to the wick. Do not focus on the yellow part of the flame since this will likely damage your eyesight.

Keep your focus on this portion and observe your mind. Take care to use an organic or natural candle, such as beeswax. Do not use a chemically produced candle since this will harm you.

Meditation is a fantastic way to calm your mind and to also ignore the negative thoughts that pop in there. I'm using such words because you'll realize that a lot of what your brain tells you is usually fear-based nonsense.

Most of the things you worry about never come to pass.

So quiet that inner voice down and allow your rational brain to come forward.

Chapter 7: Making Broader Changes

None of the things in this chapter are about confidence as much as they are about your quality of life. The truth is that a lack of confidence can be a symptom of a bad life.

Once you ask yourself the tough questions and align your life accordingly, you'll find that you will uncover a deep reservoir of confidence that no one can shake. This is because you will have tapped into what really makes you tick, and no one can take this away from you.

Purposeful Living

Do you know why you get out of bed every morning? Are you rolling out of bed to go earn a salary or are you waking up to go out there and achieve something you've always wanted to achieve?

living with a purpose doesn't necessarily mean working a job you love or some other type of ideal in your business life. As I mentioned earlier, you can work a job you don't really like and use the funds or other benefits like location to do something else that you really love doing.

My point is that instead of getting bogged down in what you do for a living, take a step back and examine how you live. Is there something at the root of your life? What gives your life meaning? A lack of confidence can be a symptom of a directionless life, a life not pursuing interests and passions.

You need to get yourself some goals and figure out what really moves you.

Forget what your friends and family are doing, what society wants from you as an ideal citizen, what image on social and traditional media is being portrayed, and find out what interests and inspires you to take action towards a better life.

What you need to do is, set your own standards, come up with your own ideal. Experiment with life and search your feelings to figure out who you are meant to be.

People usually only reassess their standards in times of great pain. They reach a breaking point where enough becomes enough and they finally snap and say this cannot go on. Why wait for your breaking point to adopt a new way of being.

Remember to adopt a Stoic view of things and accept what has happened. Now, move forward and start looking at solutions. This is where listening to your emotions is invaluable. Many of us know deep down what it is we want to do with their lives. It's just that we cover it up with all sorts of beliefs and fears and turn away from it.

If your life is in the dumps (according to you), then this is a sign that you've been ignoring your calling. I'm not saying you rush out and try to make it happen and drop everything else in the process. It's just that you need to start turning towards the direction of your goals and dreams, even if all you can do is take baby steps towards them.

A purpose is like a root in that it informs everything you do. Think of the most successful people in our society and how they behave. If you examine their behavior, you'll find that they probably say 'no' to 99% of the things that come across them so they can concentrate on the things that move the needle towards their goals.

People who suffer from a lack of confidence almost always try to do too many things that are outside the realm of their true purpose. You need to get honest with yourself and start accommodating for the time, energy and resources needed to do what you want.

Working toward your purpose takes work. You're likely to become exhausted chasing it. However, you'll find that it is worth it.

Don't worry about the 'how' and start asking yourself 'what' you want to do with your time. The answers will come to you, if you're willing to ask and search long enough.

Once you have some answers, start putting it into action and see what comes. Confidence is just one of the many positive by-products of this process.

Responsibility

Confident people take responsibility for their actions. That's a simple statement to make, but it's very difficult for most people to follow. You see, all of us like the easy life and want things to come to us a little easier.

Whether you like to admit it or not, your desire for a more carefree existence, one that avoids responsibility, is simply a product of unrealistic expectations.

People think that attaining success will lead to a care free existence, which flies in the face of how you attain and accomplish your goals. A process which requires you to take on more responsibility, these responsibilities will range from the fulfilling to the mundane but they have to be taken care of no matter what happens.

You will need to sacrifice and work to earn your dreams, and this involves undertaking truckloads of responsibility. This is a deal-breaker for most people and tails tucked between their legs, they return to their regular lives, content to work at things they don't care for.

Most people have a warped view of responsibility, they don't take seem to realize that almost everything that gets achieved requires some, and everyone wants to achieve something. If you want the body it will take responsibility, the relationship, children, money and anything else worth doing takes some responsibility.

Think of what it means to take responsibility for your words, thoughts, and actions. It means you're in control!

You should be happy in most cases to take on more responsibility, as your going to be seeing the next level of results sooner, rather than later or never.

Recognition of the fact that you govern your reactions is one of the most empowering decisions you will make in your life.

Charlie Munger has said, the best way to achieve things is to deserve them in the first place. If greater freedom and confidence is what you want, why not aim to become someone who deserves it?

Do you think someone who lashes out and blames everything on something else deserves confidence in their own abilities? Or is it the person who accepts the things that have happened to them and is still chipping away at their problems that deserves the good things in life?

Understand that responsibility and blame are two different things. In bureaucratic terms, responsibility often means uncovering who screwed up at a task. This is not what real responsibility is. The bureaucratic term is just corporate speak for a boss that wants to blame someone else.

Assume control and liberate yourself by trying to do things the right way. Victim-like behavior, looking to pass the buck, constantly feeling sorry for yourself, and being envious of others are signs of someone who does not understand responsibility and thus, lacks confidence in themselves.

Recognize your own power to change things in your life and accept that whatever has happened has no bearing on what you can do moving forward.

Take responsibility for your life and everything within your control.

Practicing Integrity

One of the hallmarks of the most admired people in our society is their code of ethics and their integrity. Integrity is a wider and less subjective umbrella, so it's worthwhile to understand this in terms of building confidence. It's not so difficult to understand why such people are highly admired. People trust them to do the right thing, and they always follow through.

Giving someone your word and then following through on it feels good. Not only do you create trust in that other person's eyes, but you can also feel the accomplishment of having done something you pledged you would do. It increases your personal power and builds your self-image.

Some people constantly give away their word for free, 'promising' things that aren't theirs to promise and 'guaranteeing' results that aren't in their control.

Would you trust such a person? At some point, don't you think the world is going to provide feedback to this person and tell them that they're untrustworthy? What will that do to their confidence levels?

I would recommend you never say that you promise, things happen around you that make it impossible to follow through. A better thing to say is 'I will try my best to' it's more realistic, and this agreement is realistically flexible, just like life is.

Integrity can require you to draw the line on issues and take a stand. It might require you to tell people things they don't like to hear. I don't mean to say that you should draw lines just to provoke people. Integrity is sticking to your values and not dropping them for personal gain.

Build integrity into everything you do and you'll find that your quality of life will improve.

This is simply because your internal scorecard will never deteriorate, and you'll realize that at the end of the day, this is the only scorecard that matters.

Becoming a person of integrity and virtues should be a constant pursuit holding even more significance than your external success. Maintaining integrity is key to keeping confidence levels at a high in the long term.

Chapter 8: Working with Your Beliefs

Implementing the things we looked at in the previous chapter is no easy task. It requires you to confront a lot of your inner demons and install new behaviors in their place. So how does one go about changing their belief systems?

You've learned what you need to deploy in order to install new habits but you don't have all the methods you need to deploy them.

This chapter is all about working with and changing your existing beliefs using some simple techniques. You have probably heard of these techniques before and have perhaps even tried them. Maybe, there were some pieces of information missing from the puzzle if they didn't work for you or maybe you just need to try again.

As you read this chapter, keep in mind that the framework of focus, repetition, emotion, and intentionality applies throughout.

Affirmations

Positive affirmations are every self-help guru's go-to technique. The problem is that a lot of affirmations don't take the self-image into account. People end up writing the most motivating and amazing affirmation statements but end up just, repeating stuff to themselves while their self-image laugh them off.

The truth is that it takes work to change your self-image via affirmations. They work for some people but don't work for others. Having said this, you should still give them a try since affirmations involve a very powerful rewiring tool: Writing.

Qualities

The qualities of a good positive affirmation are the following:

1. Present tense
2. Uses the first person
3. Is written and verbalized multiple times

The first criterion is pretty easy to understand. Your statement needs to be written as if it's a fact of your current existence. Mind you, the statement itself should ideally be process-related and not result-oriented. For example, 'I have a billion dollars' is not going to change your self-image since it is entirely result-oriented.

Instead, what are the tasks you need to complete in the short term that tie into the long term? What qualities are necessary for you to have? 'I respect my craft and work on my skills by doing x, y, and z to achieve greater success' is a far better statement since it is definitive and is process-related.

Notice how it focuses on what you need to do, not on what you want to receive. If you focus on the result, your self-image is immediately going to classify that as something it doesn't control and discard it. The result is you repeating a meaningless statement. The expertise component is more worthy of attention than the outcome.

The second quality is straight forward. Use the first person in your statements. Most people do this automatically, so this doesn't need much explanation. The last quality refers to the fact that you need to both write the statement multiple times and repeat the statement to yourself.

How many times should you do this? Well, as many times as possible with intention. Note the part about intention. You need to put all of your positive feelings behind the narration and writing of these statements so that you can wire this in quickly. Writing and repeating the statements without intention is like repeating someone else's words as far as your subconscious is concerned.

When you write your statements with intention, you'll find that you'll get fatigued after doing this a few times. This is a very good sign since it indicates that your brain is having to work to install this new neural network and that the old networks which form a part of your self-image are fighting back and contradicting the new ones.

Don't go for quantity when practicing this method. Aim for quality instead. If you find that repeating the statement is becoming a chore and that you're not able to muster enough intention, don't do it since it's a waste of time.

Something that I hinted at earlier but didn't make explicit is that your statement needs to be specific. A statement about your process needs to convey exactly what you're going to do. Hopefully, now you can see that crafting a positive affirmation is not an easy task and it isn't about copy and pasting a bunch of happy sounding quotes and reading them.

The specificity within your affirmations should be aimed at the things you will do, not what you will achieve. So if you want to enhance your public speaking skills, your affirmation should read something like 'I work for half an hour every day practicing my diction, voice modulation, and tonality to improve the way I speak.' An incorrect statement would be something like 'I'm an excellent public speaker and have no fear.'

This statement highlights another quality which is a no-no. Notice how it says 'no fear.' Well, your brain is going to read that as 'fear' and associate fear with public speaking. So, yeah, you're telling your brain that you're afraid no matter what you wrote. Always speak in the positive and don't frame your sentences as avoiding the negative. Your brain will assume the negative reality is real.

So how many statements should you write? You can have as many as you want, but for practical purposes and the fact that you need to apply intention to all of them, a maximum of three is more than enough. You'll find that crafting and reading and writing these statements will place a lot of strain on you and will cause changes in your life.

The question you're thinking of at this point might be how long will you have to wait for changes to occur? Well, research shows that it takes 21 days for the brain to learn a new habit. The true marker of a new habit is how well you react to a situation that calls for the skill. Often, you will encounter a moment where you'll automatically implement the new habit without conscious thought and only realize it later.

It is at this point that you'll realize your affirmations have been successful. A common pitfall is to skip the step that ought to come before the process of writing affirmations which is to figure out what you really want. Don't be in a rush to create change just for the sake of it. Your current situation might be unbearable for you, but this doesn't justify you doing things the wrong way around.

If you create affirmations that don't add to your true purpose, you'll find that you'll need to chop and change them around quite a bit. Avoid doing this since your brain will then classify affirmations as just another method that doesn't work. Can you write affirmations to impact your confidence in particular situations directly?

Sure you can, but remember that it needs to be process-oriented. Ultimately, confidence is an outcome so attempting to instill greater confidence via affirmations happens when you install a bigger habit of which confidence is a by-product.

Does this mean you should never focus on the outcome and only be process-oriented? Well, the next method allows you to do both.

Visualization

Here we have another method that is well-known but is almost universally practiced incorrectly. This is entirely due to error, of course, and also some ignorance. You see, most people assume they need to learn some secret sauce to figure out how to visualize well when the truth is that every single one of us is an expert at visualization.

First, let's look at the qualities of a good mental picture. It needs to be:

1. As real as possible with lots of sensory input
2. As positive as possible (not avoiding a negative)
3. Detail-oriented to make it real
4. Practiced regularly for maximum effectiveness

You might be thinking that you now need to memorize all of these line items and rigorously follow it. Well, you really don't need to. As I said, you already know how to do all of these things.

Prior Experience

Think back to a time when you suffered from anxious thoughts. What did that feel like? I'm not asking you to relive the memory, but think of the process that went into creating those thoughts. You reacted to some piece of information and created the potential negative outcomes.

It felt very real to you, and anxiety was a result of it. This is all visualization is really all about. Take whatever you did when visualizing negative results, flip it over to the positive, and you have conscious visualization all done for you. There are many different ways you can choose to visualize something.

Some people prefer to have a movie screen playing in front of them and watch a movie in which they are a character. Personally, this strikes me as being a bit impersonal but to each his own. Ultimately, you need to figure out what works for you and execute that to the best of your abilities.

Including sensory input is quite straightforward. You feel and hear and see things as you would in your ideal situation. Place yourself literally in that picture. A great way of adding sensory information is to feel the environment. So feel the breeze blowing on your skin or the heat or cold as the situation might be.

A key point to stress is to gradually add information into your picture. Don't be in a rush to add everything into it. For example, visualize the cold on your skin but hold off for now on the wolf that you're going to slay Liam Neeson style. Add that bit of information later once you're comfortable visualizing the basic details automatically.

Feeling good is a very important point when it comes to visualizing the details. You need to feel a well of positive emotion to the extent that you feel the urge to jump out of your chair and jump for joy. The stronger your positive emotion the better, so make your picture as desirable as possible.

A common question to ask is how many pictures does one need in their visualization process? Should you have one go-to picture or a bunch of related situational pictures you refer to? Well, the answer is as many as you need. Mix the aim of those pictures up as well. Have some be process-oriented and some be goal-oriented.

This is the beauty of visualization. Human beings are intensely visual creatures, and our brains cannot tell the difference between a vividly imagined picture that is made up and a true memory. When you visualize the desired outcome, your brain will take that as being real and will try to figure out the process that gives that result.

Thus, visualization engages your creative response and all you need to do at that point is to sit back and let it take over. Mind you, this doesn't mean you do nothing. The creative process is an intensely active one and you will need to take constant action to figure out what is working and what isn't and refine your process.

So, you see, while affirmations require you to know the process beforehand, you can use visualization to figure it out. So if you ever feel stuck, simply visualize. This is of great value when it comes to goal setting and achieving them. What about your beliefs, though? How can you use visualization to change them?

With some beliefs, it does pay to dig into your past and figure out how or why they came to be. The ones to do with money and relationships usually deserve such attention. Even when doing this, you should dig deep only with respect to the ones that have the most impact.

For example, if you have trouble keeping the money you make, it is worthwhile examining how your parents behaved around money. If you keep attracting malicious partners, examine what your parents' relationship was like, and you'll see the blueprint you've been following.

Your beliefs manifest as your actions, and these actions are stored in your memory. Your self-image believes it is 'like you' to behave in such a manner. Therefore, changing your beliefs is all about deactivating these neural networks that store information about your regular behavior. Visualize behaving in your desired manner and imagine yourself living out the new beliefs.

Your brain will automatically figure out what the correct beliefs need to be, and any conflicting messaging will be deactivated. Of course, this takes time, and you'll need to use the four principles of learning extensively. However, with time and repetition, you'll find your behavior changing and your results changing along with it.

So as you can see, visualization is a versatile tool for you to use. You can figure out what steps to take next as well as install behavior that you wish to manifest in real life. Just remember to focus on the positive emotions in order to speed up the process. Visualize as many times per day as you want, but don't try this when you feel fatigued or are unable to generate the required positive emotions.

Massive Action

You should have figured out by this point that creating confidence in yourself requires action. What kind of action is appropriate, though? I mean to say that you can visualize and write your affirmations, but is this enough? If you suffer from a lack of confidence in social situations, how often should you put yourself in the firing line, so to speak, and work to get over your fears?

There's no easy answer to this except to say that you should seek as much feedback as you can process. Much like how you will become fatigued after visualizing and writing your affirmations, you will reach a point where feedback will overwhelm your brain and you won't be able to process things anymore.

Sticking with the example of social situations, you might find that after a few hours of socializing you feel tired or mentally exhausted. The thing to do is to prepare for this and expect it to happen. When it does occur, you know when to take a break. Sometimes, this exhaustion will last for a few days, so don't worry about taking a small break from your practice.

This exhaustion reflects the struggle going on inside your brain where the old network is fighting back the new one. Don't worry about the new network being overwhelmed if you aren't constantly taking action; the brain doesn't work that way. However, if you refrain from taking action for too long, then your new neural networks will weaken.

All of this brings me to the topic of massive action. This has become a popular term in self-help, and there are quite a few false theories about this. Massive action as a principle is a great one, but what most people don't realize is that it is relative to the task you are performing. What is massive for you is not massive for someone else. It depends entirely on where each person is on their journey.

So how do you figure out what is massive for you? Again, there's no cut and dried logical answer for this other than to say that you need to feel your way forward. When you reach a level that's too exhausting, take a step back and maintain your position. Finding your limit is a trial and error sort of thing, and you need to be very aware of your mental state when doing this.

Massive action is NOT about motivating yourself. If you're lacking in motivation, your goals are the problem. You're not visualizing or affirming the things you want in your life enough to go do something. Examine your goals if this happens to you.

Massive action works brilliantly because, over time, you'll find that as your comfort zone expands, your ability to carry out more tasks will increase. Simply put, your brain will get used to the new regime and will accommodate a greater level of work and results. Don't try to mimic someone else's working pattern at first since this will exhaust you.

For example, don't try to work as many hours as Elon Musk claims he does per week. Instead, build your way up to it and always keep seeking feedback. There's something about feedback you need to understand. It is going to be negative at first. When you start off trying to do something new, you're going to make mistakes, and you'll thus receive negative feedback.

The problem is that people expect positive feedback for just taking action. They expect results to come pouring in immediately. It doesn't work this way. Think back to when you learned to first tie your shoelaces. You probably tied them into indecipherable knots a few times before getting it right. Every single action or behavior is going to be met with negative feedback at first; it's just the way things are.

Negative feedback is what helps you improve, so you should be welcoming it instead of shunning it as most people do. Without this information, you could not improve. When you take massive action, you're going to receive massive amounts of negative feedback. You should understand this as receiving more data so you can figure out how to do things correctly and not get emotionally attached to it.

Stop thinking in terms of 'I' and instead, think in terms of how the task needs to be done. Remove yourself from the picture and try to be as objective as possible. This is not easy to do, but with time, you'll get better at it.

The idea behind massive action is to gather as much feedback as quickly as possible so that you shorten the time it takes to start receiving positive results.

Adopt the Stoic method of focusing on the process and accept whatever comes at you. You'll find that you'll learn your lessons faster and create better results for yourself.

As human beings, we underestimate what can be done in the long term and overestimate what can be achieved in the short term. This is why it is important that you have no expectations in terms of results over the short term and instead focus solely on executing the process well over a longer time period.

Conclusion

Confidence is ultimately a by-product of living your life a certain way. While you can fake it till you make it, the reality is that you can't fake it for very long.

The way forward is to utilize the simple processes presented in the appropriate chapters in this book and working on improving your life over the long term.

The point of this book is to teach you how to build confidence within yourself, an untouchable confidence that's not dependent on the outside world's acceptance of you.

Approach your lack of confidence as an opportunity to improve your life as a whole. You have permission to be yourself, a flawed human being with massive potential to express to the world.

We are the most complex organism on the planet, likely the solar system and possibly the galaxy, the fact that you can read this and try to comprehend these words is proof that you have so much potential to share with the human race.

If you have made it this far into the book it proves you have enough focus and staying power to get things completed, you are in the 1% for something that really matters, seeing things through to completion is a trait of winners.

Most people start things but never finish them, don't stop with just reading this book you have got everything it takes to push life to the next level. Practice the things we have discussed and take your confidence to heights you didn't think were possible and most people never get to experience.

Will you take action on the things you have learned? Will you stop expecting yourself and the world to be perfect? Will you stop comparing yourself to other people? I hope you do something, it's the only way your life will improve.

I hope you are willing to try again.

Adopting Stoic practices, especially the ones highlighted in this book, will help adjust your expectations and will help you paint a more realistic picture of your future. You will be better prepared when it comes to dealing with the adversities that life throws at us.

Your results are governed by your actions and a lot of other things you cannot control

Focus on the things you can control, take some chances and learn from whatever feedback you receive.

Keep things in perspective when events move against you. You'll find that some of the negative occurrences in your life result from your own actions. Examining them is the key to not making the same mistakes again and making progress in your life.

There are a lot of reasons for you to lack confidence in today's world. Look at the presence of social media and the way mainstream news media is structured; everything is designed to pry open your insecurities and take advantage of them.

This sort of thing used to be the dominion of Hollywood exclusively, but these days, everyone is a celebrity on social media, trying to obtain your attention with negative headlines and controversial subjects. Much of this content lacks any real nuance, any real guidance towards a better life and some of it is just created to get clicks and keep your attention until the adverts are played, no matter how damaging the content is to your psyche.

Adopting the right role models goes hand-in-hand with creating a better environment for yourself, and this is crucial to improving the overall standard of your life.

Seek to consume media from people who have substance and achievement behind them.

Put your head down and focus on improving your life and confidence. Keep your blinders on and stay away from all the unnecessary negativity that sells ad space and keeps you down.

Put the work in on yourself, master your craft, your hobby,

and create the world you want to live in.

You can change your own environment and you can change yourself. Gain confidence by putting the work in and whatever else you want has a good chance to follow.

I hope reading this book has been an enjoyable experience for you, and I'm keen on hearing what you think of it. Do let me know your thoughts! I wish you the best of luck in your endeavors and all the confidence in the world.

Made in the USA
Coppell, TX
19 October 2020